"I first met Alisha during her days as president of the Georgia Youth & College Division of the NAACP as she became active with the Georgia Coalition for the People's Agenda. She is a gifted and energetic young woman, and we expect to hear great things from her for years to come. I have much admiration for her high degree of civic consciousness. I expect all of us to find a rich and rewarding experience in reading *No Apologies.*"—**Reverend Dr. Joseph Lowery,** "Dean" of the American civil rights movement, Presidential Medal of Freedom recipient

"Alisha Thomas Morgan is a dynamic leader, who, like so many Spelman women, has made a choice to change the world! She has found her voice, and it is powerful. She is a woman to watch in the years ahead!"—**Beverly Tatum,** PhD, President of Spelman College

Kojo Brenda, Kathy,
Thanks for your support.
Continue to lead and serve.
Make No Apologies for it.
Alisha T. Mog

NO APOLOGIES

POWERFUL LESSONS IN LIFE, LOVE & POLITICS

ALISHA THOMAS MORGAN

authorHOUSE®

AuthorHouse™
1663 Liberty Drive
Bloomington, IN 47403
www.authorhouse.com
Phone: 1-800-839-8640

Book Production:
Executive Assistant to Alisha Thomas Morgan: Jarrett Hill
Photographer: James Anthony (cover and back flap photos)
Makeup Artist: Jon Stevens

Inside Photography: A special thanks to the following:
Office of Sonny Perdue, Governor of the State of Georgia
Office of David Ralston, Speaker of the Georgia House of
Representatives& Chris R. Williams, PhD, photographer

First published by AuthorHouse   8/26/2010

ISBN: 978-1-4520-2088-4 (e)
ISBN: 978-1-4520-2087-7 (sc)
ISBN: 978-1-4520-2086-0 (hc)

Library of Congress Control Number: 2010906685

Printed in the United States of America

This book is printed on acid-free paper.

To David, Lailah-bug, Rashaan, my parents, Mama Morgan and D,
Grandma Josephine Thomas, my constituents of District 39, and all the
courageous leaders who have dedicated their lives to service

CONTENTS

Acknowledgments

I could not have written this book without the sacrifices, love, and friendship of the following people who pushed me to keep fighting the good fight. Thank you for all that you are and all you mean to me.

To the love of my life, David L. Morgan Jr., for inspiring me to be a better person and for being a loving and supportive husband and incredible father.

To my mother, who poured everything she had into me, and to my father, who taught me the importance of hard work.

To Dr. Joseph Lowery for being the ultimate servant leader.

To Tharon Johnson, Rashad Taylor, Heather Fatzinger, Yunice Emir, and Ebony Barley for believing in the impossible and being my kitchen cabinet.

To Michael Brewer and the rest of "team Morgan" for always having my back.

To Clyde Anderson for starting me on my way through this journey, and to Anton Gunn for your great advice.

To Pastor Purvis for being my friend, mentor, and pastor.

To all of the nameless faces on whose shoulders I stand.

INTRODUCTION

I 'VE BEEN IN ELECTED OFFICE since 2003. I've had the opportunity to experience a great deal in my life that has helped shape who I am and how I see the world. That view makes me a better public servant and helps me empathize with those who experience hardship. Of all of my life experiences, the greatest lessons for me have come in politics. Most of my lowest lows and some of my highest highs have come from the twists and turns of the political and legislative process. The most important lesson I've learned is to never apologize for who I am. I am that way because that's who God made me to be. I don't make apologies for my upbringing, no matter how dysfunctional it was at times, or for the tremendous opportunities I was afforded to be exposed to so much.

I make no apologies for the decisions I've made—the good or the bad. Not that I wouldn't make decisions differently when presented with the same dilemma, but I understand that those bad decisions were filled with life lessons that have helped shape who I am, how I handle adversity, and, just as importantly, how I can help other people who face the same challenge. I have also learned never to apologize for my convictions. Although I can often be misunderstood, apologizing or simply remaining silent isn't an option.

Living life unapologetically does not come without consequences. I've lost relationships and even had my heart broken. But out of those experiences comes a real understanding of who I am and the life I am destined to live. My time thus far in public service has taught me more than how to navigate the political and legislative processes. It has better prepared me to navigate through life. It has taught me how to communicate with people who are different from me, how to deal with conflict, how to compromise a position without losing my values, and how to build relationships with people.

No Apologies is a way of life. It's not just my unwillingness to be silenced on issues that are important to me. I refuse to apologize for the values I have, the things I want for myself and family, and the things I want for you. Many of us live apologetic lives because we are afraid of standing out, of being ostracized, of not getting that promotion, of people knowing who we really are. If we stop and think about the people who have made significant contributions to the world, we can see that they did so because they were not afraid. We know them because they were willing to stand out, to do something first, to say it louder, or to create something that didn't exist before. There is a great quote by historian and Harvard professor Laurel Thatcher that says, "Well-behaved women seldom make history." We don't remember a woman who is seen and not heard. We don't remember the people who go along to get along and do just enough to stay under the radar. Living an unapologetic life is not just about taking risks or not being afraid. Living an unapologetic life is about standing strong in your convictions and setting standards for yourself, your family, and your community.

What happens when we say we're sorry? We acknowledge that we have made a mistake, that we have done something or someone wrong. When we say we're sorry, we weaken our own power, especially when we know what we are doing is right. Sorry says, "I've hurt you and I don't want to do it again." Sorry is admitting fault. How are we at fault when we stand up for children who have no voice? How are we at fault when we demand change in a public education system that is broken? How are we guilty of something when we refuse to accept that our upbringing, our past, determines our future? Why say you're sorry when you are the only person who has the courage to speak up at work, when no one else has the guts to do so? When we apologize for doing what we believe is right, we acquiesce to those in power, diminishing our own voice and the voices of others who want to stand with us.

Where would we be as a country if Rosa Parks had apologized for refusing to give up her seat on that Montgomery bus? What would history say about her if she had apologized and said she would never do it again? What if all black people had decided that Jim Crow laws were acceptable and that we just needed to go along to get along? What if women had decided that they would accept not having the right to vote? They would have been apologizing for who God made them to be and accepting second-class citizenship. We can never apologize for being black, female, young, old, gay, or whoever God made us. When you see injustice and do nothing, say nothing, and ignore that feeling in your gut that tells you to speak, you are saying, "I'm sorry."

We cannot apologize for being who we are and being the sum of our experiences. We cannot apologize for how we arrived at this destination, no matter what it is. We must not apologize because we are poor or of means. We must not apologize for standing up or speaking out. We cannot apologize for our actions when we are standing for what's right or fair. We must not apologize for speaking truth to power, saying the things that need to be said even when it makes people feel uncomfortable. We must not apologize for doing what's right because we are afraid of the consequences. We must not apologize because we are afraid that we will miss out on the promotions at our jobs or special favors we used to get.

We must never apologize for making the power structure uncomfortable or forcing a shift in the status quo. We must never apologize for going against the establishment, even if it includes our friends. We must never apologize for exercising courage and forcing people to look at themselves. We must never apologize for being who we are because we are afraid that we will end up by ourselves.

We must always stand on the side of justice and take whatever consequences might be handed down. Why? Because that's how change is made. That is how we force those who are in power to do what is right, even when they don't want to, even when they don't understand it or agree that it's the right thing to do. Never apologize for standing on principle or being a voice for those who lack one.

What we need are more individuals and communities with a no-apologies attitude, those who have said, "I'm sick and tired of being sick and tired, and I'm not taking it anymore." We need our little boys to make no apologies for setting their dreams beyond a rap song or a basketball. We need our girls to make no apologies for refusing to give up their bodies too fast because they want to be loved. We need communities to step out of complacency and speak out on their own behalf. We need some "I'm standing up for what I believe in and not saying sorry" kind of spirit that will help move our communities, and thus our country, forward.

Make no mistake, living a life with no apologies certainly comes with consequences. I am a black woman, one of the youngest elected officials in the entire state of Georgia, and I represent a district in a county that is predominantly white and Republican. Cobb County had never had an African American serve in the legislature before I did. I also serve in a legislature that is mostly older, male, and white. I had to learn early that my purpose for being in the legislature was not to try to blend in or become a seat warmer while things happened all around me. I knew my voice and my perspective were important, and I wasn't going to apologize for being different.

Speaking up can be uncomfortable and, in some instances, isolating. At the same time, it earns many admirers who wish they had the heart to do the same thing. I want to encourage you not to be afraid to speak up and not to apologize for it. The rewards of empowering people and creating change for people who will never know your name outweigh the frustrations over the few who refuse to stand for anything because they are more concerned with being liked than doing what's right. I hope this book will encourage you to continue to stand firm. We need you. We need more strong voices who are willing speak up, misbehave, and maybe even make a little history.

This book comes from my heart, as does everything I do. Every day we are blessed to live on this earth, lessons abound. It's up to us to stop and take in what life and our experiences are teaching us. It's not always about mistakes either. Sometimes we think the only time we learn something is from a negative experience. There are lessons in everything we do and what other people do. Looking for the lessons helps us to be connected with ourselves and provides us the sacred opportunity to constantly seek to better who we are as individuals and as a community. My prayer is that this book will be a blessing to you, whether you are hoping to enter the political arena or just want to live a more fulfilled life. We have to be intentional about wanting to be the best that we can be. If, today, you didn't give your best, tomorrow provides another opportunity. We can keep trying, keep learning, and keep getting better.

There are lessons in every experience that you have, even if they are just reminders or confirmations of what you already know. Take the time to learn and receive the lessons in your life. The lessons that I leave at the end of each chapter have really helped me in my journey in the political arena. Although politics is ever-changing and very fluid, these lessons are constant. These lessons aren't just for people in politics either. They can be used in almost any situation you may find yourself in. Situations will change; it's your values and integrity that shouldn't. The dilemmas you face are the same ones I face. We are challenged to maintain who we are at the core in the midst of our pursuits in life.

This book is not about how perfect life can be. In fact, I talk about the mistakes I have made as well as the things that I have done well. Our most important life lessons come from both. Every day that goes by I am still learning new lessons. I should. You should, too. You may not be a politico who watches MSNBC or FOX News; maybe you can't even name your local elected officials—although I hope you will be inspired enough by this book to want to know that and get involved.

This book is for the daughter who carries too many of her parents' burdens; it's for the employee who can't help speaking up at work. It's for the student in college who thought she needed permission to lead and the lawyer who struggles with choosing civil rights over corporate law. It's for the person who sees life a little differently from everybody else and wants to feel comfortable in his or her own skin. It's also for the curious person who wants to know why a young black woman in the Georgia legislature thought she needed to write a book. It's for the amazing young women I meet when I'm traveling who have the fire in their eyes to create change and make a mark in the world but need an extra push.

This book is for my big sisters Heather Fatzinger, Nataki Osborne, Heather Hudson, Sharon Lettman, Deane Bonner, Shirley Franklin, and Helen Butler, women who have inspired me, taught me, and led by example. This book is for my little sisters Jessica Carter, Lekisha Harris, Nekpen Osuan, Quandra Muomah, Zandria Mims, Jasmine Walker, Kristin Goss, and other young women whose lives I am blessed enough to sow seeds in. (You too, brother Michael Brewer.) This book is for sisters and brothers I hope to meet one day who will find the life lessons in this book impacting enough to apply to their lives. Whoever you are and wherever you are, open yourself to the lessons in this book that can be used at any stage in your life. May the words that come from my heart inspire you to be better than you were before you opened the pages of this book. May you live your life to the fullest and take the time to learn all of the great lessons along the way.

1. NO APOLOGY

I T WAS A SATURDAY MORNING. It was the first time we had ever
been in session on a Saturday and the first time for Family Day
at the capitol. It was an idea of the Republicans, who had just taken
the reins of leadership in the Georgia House and Senate. Democrats
had controlled the House, Senate, and governor's office for 130 years.
Republicans had been the minority party for so long that they had
plenty of time to think of all the new things they wanted to do, and I
guess Family Day was one of them. This was a time when they could all
bring their families down to the capitol to show off their new power. It
was their way of taking them for a ride in their brand new car.

It was already tense in the House, where I served. We were toward
the end of our forty-day session, and we Democrats were still licking
our wounds and digesting the fact that there was a new sheriff in town
with new rules. Some of those rules were downright unfair, put in place
to make sure the Democrats would never have access to power again.
Some rules determined how much time we were allowed to speak on
a bill; others restricted any Democratic voice in the legislative process.

We had enough to be angry about; add to that the kinds of issues that we were taking up.

Just the night before we'd voted on the infamous Voter ID bill. In Georgia, the Voter ID law eliminated a list of seventeen different forms of identification used for in-person voting and narrowed the list down to six. It eliminated identification like student IDs from private colleges (like Spelman, the college I attended), work IDs from nongovernmental jobs, and social security cards. This was the new bill in the Republican playbook that year that was introduced in several states after it was successfully passed in the home of Dr. Martin Luther King Jr.

I remember the night before Family Day as if it were last night. We were having one of our marathon sessions where we were in for ten to twelve hours straight. This was the perfect environment to bring up a bill that didn't go through the proper legislative process. The state senate had just voted on this same bill, and we'd heard that the black Senators had debated the bill and walked out of the chamber when the bill passed. Just fifteen minutes after we heard about it, it was the black House members' turn to address this issue on the House floor. I hadn't heard anything about the bill and didn't know its contents. I knew that it had to do with voting, and it must have been pretty contentious for the black Senators to walk out of session as a result.

None of us had time to digest what was in the bill before it was called and the debate began. One by one, members of the black caucus in the house went up to the well—the podium in the chamber where legislators make their speeches. They talked about the importance of voting, making sure the process was accessible to all people, and gave accounts of their own painful experiences growing up during the Jim Crow era. I didn't have any Jim Crow experiences to call upon, but I had plenty of experiences in the NAACP, where I had learned about Jim Crow and the struggle of black people to finally exercise our constitutional right in this country. As a high school student, I had met Rosa Parks and Jesse Jackson through the NAACP. I spoke from my heart and urged the members of the legislature to vote against this bill and look more carefully at how people attempt to restrict access to the ballot. It was no accident that these requirements were only for in-person voters and that there were no photo identification requirements at all for voters who voted absentee by mail.

Legislators who represented rural communities joined in the opposition, because they knew that their constituents would have a hard time voting in person; if they didn't have one of the six identification forms on the list, they would have to buy one. For them, it amounted to a poll tax, a tactic that black voters knew all too well in the South. To no avail, the bill passed along racial and party lines. Most Democrats voted against the bill; the Republicans voted for it. Even some Republicans who didn't agree with the bill felt pressured to vote for it, because this was an important issue for the Republicans.

The black members and a few white Democrats walked out in protest of the vote. As at any other time when issues come up that focus on race, there was much tension in the chamber. Race is already an uncomfortable issue that most people don't like to discuss. Here was a bill that we knew would have an adverse impact on the poor, students, and people of color, because they would not have easy access to this restrictive list of ID forms. I remember going home that night feeling so frustrated. With all of the issues we needed to address, we were spending tax dollars creating a solution that was waiting for a problem. There was the Voter ID bill, the new rules, the new leadership, and the feeling that we were back on a slave plantation. These things caused all of us to feel tense and frustrated. They conjured up negative thoughts and frustrations, and distracted us from doing the real work of the people.

The next morning was Family Day. We had been in session late the night before, and now we had to come back for the dog-and-pony show the new leadership wanted to put on for their families. Before I got to the capitol, I joined hundreds of people from around the state who came to participate in a march from the baseball stadium to the state capitol. It was our way to make our voices heard on the many issues that weren't being addressed. I marched with the group to the capitol and went inside to take my seat. The whole time I was feeling heavy-hearted. My spirit wasn't at peace. I had something to say about what had happened the night before, and my soul wasn't going to rest until I got it off my heart. It's in those moments that I know I can't have peace until I speak up.

So I did. I signed up to do a morning order, which is an allotted time members are given for what could be considered points of personal privilege. We have the opportunity to say whatever we want to say. Oftentimes legislators use this as an opportunity to welcome a group to the capitol or talk about a bill working through the process. Some use it to talk about current events happening in the state or in the world. Under the new rules, the Speaker of the House assigned each speaker a certain amount of time. On this particular day, we each had two minutes and thirty seconds.

The first legislator went up for her morning order to honor her maid for Women's History month. She went on and on beyond her two minutes and thirty seconds, talking about how much this woman had impacted her life and how she had sacrificed so much to have the life she now had. When she went over her time and the Speaker did not react, I figured, because it was Family Day, he wasn't going to stick with the time constraints. Finally, she finished and she took her seat.

Then the second legislator got up. He welcomed all of the families to their state capitol and delighted in how wonderful it was to have all of them there. Coincidentally, those hundreds of people who had marched from the stadium to the capitol were locked out of the capitol and told that the building was already at capacity. Some of the legislators were working to try to get them in, but with no success. The second speaker never acknowledged those who didn't make it into the building, but went on welcoming members of the public who did make it into the House chamber. He, too, went on for more than his two minutes and thirty seconds, which confirmed to me that the Speaker was relaxing the rule because, after all, it was Family Day.

Finally, his speech was over and it was my turn. I was filled with emotion from the night before. I felt sad, frustrated, angry, powerless, and even oppressed. My soul was stirring, and I needed to speak and say what was on my heart. I needed to talk about the elephant in the room from the night before, and I refused to allow myself to be ignored or brushed to the side. I knew this was one of the times I had to speak "truth to power." That is, I had to say what needed to be said, whether other people had the guts to say it or not. Speaking truth to those in power, in this instance, meant recalling what had happened the night before and addressing the questions from my colleagues about why I "get so emotional" when I and others go to the well to speak on voting. I needed to say these things to those who were in power, in this case the Republicans, and inform them that I was not going to sit idly by and allow this effort to turn back the clock on voting rights and say or do nothing.

This was one of those moments where you may not be able to do anything, but you certainly have your voice; and it was vital that those in power heard it. While other legislators never acknowledged what had happened the night before, my soul wasn't going to rest unless I did. I took to the well and recalled for the chamber what had happened the night before. I reminded the audience that my people had come to this country in chains and that we weren't going back. I recalled the moment I met Rosa Parks. I recalled how I felt when I watched the *Eyes on the Prize* videos as a high school student and was inspired to speak my own truth to power. I talked about the many shoulders on which I stand, from Fannie Lou Hamer to Shirley Chisholm and many others. I called the names of our ancestors and even reminded them about Bishop Henry McNeal Turner, who was expelled from the legislature, along with thirty-two other African Americans, because of the color of their skin.

By that time, I am sure I was over two minutes and thirty seconds, but time was no longer a factor for me. Call it being lost in the moment; call it defying authority. Call it putting my degree in drama to use. Call it what you want, but I was experiencing a moment with the ancestors, and time was not my concern. I do remember hearing the Speaker's gavel get louder and louder. I remember the room getting quiet and tense. People wondered what would happen next: *What is this new Speaker going to do to control his chamber?* I remember two guys walking up to each side of me, perhaps to remove me. The gavel got louder and louder. "Representative Morgan, your time has expired."

There was nothing that could be done, because this was the moment. I hadn't planned it, didn't know it would happen, but this was the moment that decorum and the status quo needed to be challenged. This was the moment that no gavel, house rules, or anything else could keep me from speaking out. As the gavel got louder and louder and the Speaker's face turned a tomato shade of red, I finished my morning order by singing "Ain't Gonna Let Nobody Turn Me Around." I sang, "I'm gonna keep on walkin', keep on talkin', marchin' up to freedom land!" And then, I took my seat.

There was applause from the gallery. The Speaker made a comment about other members being civilized in the chamber. It was all he could do to recover from his public embarrassment. It was a whirlwind after that. There were rumors that the leadership was looking for ways to expel me from the legislature. At first, that sounded scary, until I realized I would be in great company. The last person who was expelled from the Georgia legislature was my NAACP colleague, Julian Bond, for his stance against the Vietnam War. Then, of course, there were the thirty-three African Americans who were expelled because of the color of their skin. The truth is, fear was never a factor. I had never felt so free and connected to something bigger than myself. That moment wasn't about my passionate speech. It was about standing up and not standing down. That moment was about challenging the status quo and reminding folk that we are not appointed to places to take up space or to wait for someone else to speak up. That moment became one of the most defining moments in my life.

That weekend, I was getting all kinds of calls. The Speaker wanted a public apology. The leadership was now discussing a public reprimand. I think they knew an expulsion was exactly what they didn't need to do to the youngest serving member of the legislature from Cobb County, who had started out as a community organizer.

The hardest part of this experience was getting the calls from my colleagues in the legislature. One by one, they would call or, on that Monday, pull me to the side and share all kinds of stories. One legislator shared a story about her family at the height of the civil rights movement. They were on a road trip when they got stopped by the police. Her father, who was strong and powerful to their family, was suddenly weak and feeble when talking to the police. He wouldn't look the officer in the eyes and stood with his head down as the officer spoke to him. The legislator asked her dad about his behavior when he got back in the car. Her dad explained to her that it was important to respect authority and to do whatever you needed to do to get through the situation.

I wasn't sure whether she was telling me that I should have allowed the harsh rules and injustice to go on unchecked, or that I needed to apologize for speaking my truth to the Speaker. Whatever she was trying to get across to me, I couldn't get it. I couldn't understand the moral of her story. I never looked at her or many other legislators like her in the same way. The leadership in my own party sent everyone they could to convince me that an apology was in order. They sent legislators I considered my friends and mentors, and those who were well-respected. They all felt I needed to make an apology for my actions—and a public apology at that.

This moment was defining because they even sent the "activists" of the legislature. Most legislators just want to serve, pass a few bills, and not make too much noise or bring attention to themselves. There are others who live for the fight. They see a good legislative fight and they run toward it—and then to the media and anyone else they can get to listen. They will call for a press conference, a march, and any other forum to call attention to the injustice. These are the activists who aren't willing to just go along to get along.

I had been considered one of them. After this incident, I was in a category all by myself. One activist legislator even pulled me aside to another room to lecture me about leaving that activist stuff on the outside. His message was that, while on the inside, we are not to break the decorum. Legislative bodies are steeped in traditions and decorum. It's how you dress, the lingo you use when in the legislative chamber. It's how the agenda flows. It's how business has been done for decades. He said you can make noise all you want on the outside, but on the inside, whether you like it or not, it's not "appropriate" to break decorum.

Let's think about that for a moment. Jim Crow wasn't just the decorum in our country; it was the law of the land. Can you imagine where we would be if the students in North Carolina and many other places had decided it was not "appropriate" to break the law by sitting down at a "public" lunch counter? What if Rosa Parks had said she would give up her seat on that Alabama bus because she didn't want to break decorum? What about the hundreds of courageous young people who weren't afraid to go to jail, who set out to register black people to vote? What if they said they weren't going to conduct registration drives because they didn't want to break decorum?

This was such a difficult time for me. So many "influential" legislators were trying to convince me that I was wrong. I started second-guessing myself. Then I paused for just a moment, in the midst of the mayhem, and relied on a life lesson that my mother had taught me years ago: Consider the source. I realized that not one person waiting outside of that House chamber had criticized my actions or encouraged an apology. Instead, they smiled, hugged me and thanked me for standing up and shedding light on what was happening in the legislature. Only members of the legislature had come, one by one, trying to make their cases for me to apologize.

While it was one of the loneliest times in my entire life, I had to learn to trust my heart and instinct, as well as my purpose for being elected *for a time such as this*. I was lonely because I didn't feel like I had any colleagues around me who really understood my struggle or could help me deal with the consequences of the aftermath. There were some who said, whether I chose to apologize or not, they would be with me. But no one sat down with me and said, "This is how we move forward; this is how we use this opportunity to make the process better; here is how you can respond to this situation." I had no one to go to.

At that moment, it was important for me to grow personally and politically. This was early on in my public service life, and I had a feeling this wouldn't be the only moment I would challenge the status quo. It forced me to take stock of what I have and who I am. It made me think hard about why I was there in the first place. It also gave me a taste of what it would be like whenever I had the courage to stand, even when no one else did. We talk about being willing to stand in that moment, when no one else is there to have our backs, but how do we handle it? What do we do? That moment I had to think about all of those things. It's moments like this that teach us the most important lessons in life.

The most telling part of this incident was watching the public reaction versus the reaction of my colleagues. Days afterwards, I would walk into the chamber and very few people would even speak to me. There were very few smiles or the usual casual conversations; people were afraid to associate with me. I will never forget how I felt during that time. I will never forget the loneliness that I felt. I could talk to the activists on the outside, but they couldn't relate to the consequences of my actions on the inside. I couldn't talk to my colleagues, because the ones who supported me weren't jumping at the opportunity to really *do* anything. They supported me because they are my friends. I appreciated that, but I knew that *I* was all I had at that moment.

For the next few days, I listened to people, one by one, who had their own ways of trying to convince me to apologize for my actions. The more I heard from people, the more I realized that an apology—and especially a public apology—was the last thing I needed to do. Instead I needed to use that moment to shed light on all the wrongs taking place in the process. I used each television and newspaper interview to talk about things like the Hawk system—a newly implemented committee system that guaranteed votes from an already heavily-Republican majority and allowed the speaker to appoint *"ex officio"* committee members during a bill hearing, on the spot, to guarantee that the vote would go his way. It was the silencing of our voices, and they were calling it the new legislative process. My situation was difficult and lonely, but speaking out was necessary and critical.

I did speak to non-legislators who were adamant about not apologizing. When I considered who they were, I became more determined that an apology for my actions—public or not—was not an option. The best piece of advice I received was unsolicited. It was from an older gentleman who was a lobbyist and a member of the clergy. He said that, if people talked about a public reprimand for not apologizing, I should "wear it like a badge of honor." I'll never forget that moment. I smiled, and he smiled. My decision was made; I wasn't apologizing, no matter what the consequences.

I went to the People's Agenda meeting that day. This is a coalition of civil rights and social justice organizations convened by Dr. Joseph Echols Lowery. Dr. Lowery is a national icon in his late eighties whose history goes back to working alongside Dr. King. His most recent notable moments were at the funeral of Coretta Scott King, where he courageously challenged President George W. Bush on fighting the Iraq war by "sending smart bombs on dumb missions"—all through poetry. He gave the benediction at the inauguration of President Barack Obama, where he called attention to the racism that still exists in our country; and, most recently, he was awarded the nation's highest civilian honor bestowed by the president, the Medal of Freedom. Dr. Lowery is a fearless civil rights activist whom I greatly respect, not only because of the many sacrifices he's made for me and millions of others, but also because he is not intimidated by young leadership. In fact, he encourages it. He had the vision in the late nineties to convene all of the civil, human, women's workers, and youth advocacy groups; he encouraged them to report to one another on the work they were each doing for voter empowerment and to work together in coalition rather than competition. We still meet weekly.

I walked into the meeting to a standing ovation. There was a sense of pride in the room because, finally, somebody had spoken up. I had a moment to address the crowd and told them I was scheduled to meet with the Speaker while he contemplated how to handle his public embarrassment. A short while into the meeting, I had to leave for my appointment with him.

Before I could sit down and get very deep into the meeting, an aide interrupted to give the Speaker and one of his team members a note. He quietly exited the room and reentered with the look of death in his eyes. He had met with Dr. Joseph Lowery and several others in the lobby. They had shown up on their own to demand that the Speaker leave me alone. I don't know what was said, exactly, or if that was the deciding moment, but I never heard a word about expulsion or a public reprimand.

The Speaker did take to the well one day that week and attempt to scold me indirectly. He was free to say what he wanted, but the truth had won out.

After that, the Speaker even threatened to limit the number of times I took to the well to speak. I welcomed that gesture, as it would only prove his dictator-like style at the time, one that limited speech and diverse thought. I believe that, after he thought about things a little more, he changed his mind. I never got turned down when requesting to speak. However, the next legislative session, they did install what is now called the "Morgan switch." That allows the Speaker to turn off the microphones at his discretion. That's okay, too. Remember, creating change is a game of chess, not checkers. If I were ever to challenge the Speaker again, it wouldn't be from the well.

Although that was one of the most difficult moments in my life, it was one of the most important, because I was reminded about my own purpose for serving in the legislature. It taught me the importance of planning and how to build upon what may have started as a tactic but needed to become a part of an entire strategy. I also got a hard lesson in what happens when you are part of the institution too long, referring to some of my colleagues whom I (and many others, for that matter) had expected to stand with me. I learned that I could come through more difficult moments, even when I had only me to depend on; I would still make it just fine.

It was from that experience that we coined the title of this book. One of the hardest moments of my life became one of the most important. It was a defining, life-shaping experience that, at the time, seemed almost unbearable but is now a part of my story. When you understand what you have been called to do, and you must do difficult things that are hard for others to understand, you must not apologize. When you are standing in the gap for others, understanding that the consequences of your actions can be grave, you still must not apologize. When you understand that the consequences of *not* acting are even more severe, an apology is not an option. People won't always understand it, and many won't always agree with it. If it's who you are and who God called you to be, apologizing is not an option.

❈ Lessons I Learned Along the Way ❈

1. Never apologize for standing up for what you believe in. It's so easy to sit back and watch instead of speak up when you see wrong. We have good reason to remain silent. Often the people who are courageous enough to speak up are faced with great opposition and consequences. If you think about any change that's been made in the world, it's because someone did speak up. He or she understood that the benefits of speaking up outweighed the consequences that come with it. Stand up for what you believe. We are called to speak for those who have no voice. When we are afraid to stand, we silence our voice and the voices of others. If you don't speak, then who will? Be bold, stand up, and make no apologies.

2. Consider the source. So often we get caught up in what people say, what they think we should be doing, how someone would feel if we took a certain action. Before you decide that you will take advice, listen to the haters, or give any credence to what is being said, always consider the source. Is this someone who has your best interest at heart, someone who wants the best for you? Is this someone who is on your level? Does he or she understand your calling? We can't always accept what *everybody* has to say. Have the discernment to determine whom you should listen to and whose words you allow to affect you.

3. Speak truth to power. If you are reading this book, chances are you have been called to serve and to advocate for those who don't have a voice. Sometimes you must speak the truth to a power that is a deserved enemy. Sometimes the power is your friend. Whoever the power is, we must not ever be afraid or ashamed to speak truth to them. Speaking truth to power is often hard to do, because we don't want to make people feel uncomfortable; we want to be liked; and, sometimes, we just don't want to be the one to rock the boat. Speaking truth to power is never about you. It's about the people you must speak for—their cause, their plight, and their issues that are bigger than us.

4. Be prepared. Once you decide you will challenge the status quo or use your voice to speak truth to power, make sure you have a plan in place that takes into account what the consequences are. Be ready for whatever the response will be so that you are moved by your mind, not your emotion. Think through the courses of action ahead of time. You won't always know how the opposition—or even your friends—will react, but make sure you have considered the possibilities and how you will respond. This requires some strategy and thought ahead of time so that you won't be caught with your guard down.

2. GREAT PREPARATION

So, WHO AM I? How did I become unapologetic for who I am? I was born in Hollywood, Florida, and raised in Miami. I grew up with both of my parents in the house, along with my brother, who is four years older than me. My mother was the one who took interest in my development and put me into everything imaginable. I was in tap, jazz, ballet, baton twirling, Girl Scouts, and a few girls' leadership programs; I even played the violin, piano, and flute. Let my dad tell it, it was all for about five minutes each. My mother is an example of the importance of parental involvement, not just in school, but in the life of a child. She hadn't always been involved, because she was a nurse and often worked long, late shifts. When she did discover the importance of involvement, it was just in time, as I, like many pre-teens, could have headed down the wrong track. Instead, those classes, the structure and discipline of dance, the competition and travel, the development of social skills, and the overall exposure to so many things have all played an integral role in who I am today.

My father didn't value those things as much. He valued working and providing for our family. For all of my life, up until recently, my father worked three jobs, seven days a week. It was common for him to be gone all day and to return in the evening from one of his three jobs. My mom worked multiple jobs, particularly while I attended Spelman College. My mother gave me everything she had to ensure that I would be successful and not become one of the statistics. My father gave the best he could. For him, that was a roof over my head and food on the table. From my mother I learned patience, perseverance, and unconditional love. From my father I learned the importance of a strong work ethic.

One of the most beneficial decisions Mom made was to drag me to a Miami Dade Youth Council NAACP meeting. I remember it was one January night in 1994. I was a freshman in high school, and she came home and told me to put my shoes on because we were going to the NAACP meeting. I didn't even know what NAACP meant at the time. It sounded boring, so I grabbed a book to take along with me. I was sure that this was a group of old people who would be sitting around a room, complaining about the issues of the day, and talking about things that had nothing to do with me.

Lucky for me, I was wrong. I walked into the meeting, and the room was filled with young people. A young person was running the meeting, and young people were taking notes, discussing the agenda and issues. I was sold. I was fascinated that young people were running their own meeting, and it appeared that the adults in the room were there for support. It's the thing I love most about the NAACP. It is not only a notion, but written in the constitution of the NAACP: that youth councils and college chapters are equal—in terms of status, rights, and power—to speak out on issues with no need for permission from the adult branch or college chapter. Like every other unit, adult or not, young people were empowered, not as leaders of tomorrow, but leaders in that very moment.

Needless to say, I never opened the book I'd brought. Instead I was inspired. I was moved by the opportunity to plan things and speak out on issues that were important to me as a young person and not have someone look down on me or tell me that I didn't know what I was talking about.

My real introduction to the national NAACP was the year when I ran for Ms. NAACP. Attracted to the pageantry of it, I garnered over three hundred youth members, which was the real purpose of the competition. After winning the state and first runner-up nationally, I was hooked on NAACP for both the social and political experiences I was having. I later rose to become the president of the youth council, graduated high school, and eventually became the president of the Spelman College chapter, even serving as the state president for the Georgia Youth and College Division.

The NAACP played a significant role in shaping my ideals about being black in America, defining who I am, and developing my passion and purpose to serve and empower others. Dr. Shirley Johnson, the youth advisor in Miami, would always remind us, "NAACP is not a social club." Given that she grew up in Mississippi and was close to the family of Medgar Evars, a voting rights pioneer who was slain in his own driveway, she believed that NAACP was a way of life and way to make life better for all people. She and other strong women within the youth council and the organization were constant reminders of how much the NAACP had done for African Americans, and they often reminded us how much more we still owed to it. I can't recall any other experience, including formal education, where I learned more about African American history, was more inspired about my history, or had the opportunity to help shape history as a young person. I am forever grateful to the organization that empowered me and other young people, teaching us to be leaders today, rather than tomorrow.

That's where I developed the audacity to believe that young people are very much capable of leading. That early lesson left quite the indelible mark on my life that has helped me to see myself as equally capable, equipped, and empowered as any adult or—after I came into adulthood—any older person. It was not meant to ignore the wisdom and experience older adults had to share. It was simply a place to start from, one that did not dictate that I start two steps behind. Unfortunately, I find this foundation is often untapped within the NAACP. We still have to remind young people within the organization of their own power. When you understand your role, you are much more likely to hit the ground running and use the power you have to create the kind of change you want to see.

I attended a performing arts junior high school for theater. When it was time to audition for New World, the performing arts high school, all of my friends and I were getting our monologues prepared, rehearsing, and getting ready to embark on a performing arts path we believed we would follow long after high school. They all got their acceptance letters, and I got a rejection letter. I was distraught and could not understand why. Instead I attended a magnet school that had a performing arts focus. I attended that large high school for one year and made sure that I was ready for my audition the second time around, because I knew New World was the place for me to be.

I re-auditioned and was accepted the second time. I attended and graduated from New World with a focus in musical theatre. I had tremendous opportunities at New World to perform and even direct my first play, which was a great success. I also experienced some of my highest highs and lowest lows in terms of my performance abilities at that school. I auditioned for the traveling performing group with all of my friends. You guessed it—they all got in, and I didn't. I will never forget the director of the program telling me not to worry because one day I was going to be president. At the time I thought she was just patronizing me, but I would later realize that she saw something in me that I couldn't see yet.

It worked out fine, though. They had their performing group after school and weekends, and I had the experience of working in television as a young television personality on a show called *By Kids for Kids*. It was a show created by the local ABC affiliate that gave young people like me the opportunity to learn all sides of television production. I learned how to create news stories, how to edit, and even had the honor of interviewing gospel singer Shirley Caesar. What incredible exposure I had. It was such a great experience that I pondered going into the television industry. Along with my television gig and other extracurricular activities, I stayed involved with the NAACP.

I didn't abandon theater. Now I had two passions: theater and social justice. I knew from being involved in the NAACP that I had a responsibility to serve and to speak up for those who needed a voice. I now had the tools and a structure in place to support those things I wanted to do in the community. Ironically, at school, I became the only person out of my group of friends, and one of two in the entire school, to become a finalist in a national theater contest for acting during my senior year. It was another indication that my path would be unique.

During the spring of 1996, my senior year, it was time for college applications. I visited Spelman in Atlanta and had fallen in love. Even though I'd been sure I was going to Howard from the time I was a freshman in high school, once I stepped foot on Spelman's campus, I knew it would be the place that I could call home. I applied to Spelman, Clark Atlanta University, Howard, and Florida A&M University. In keeping with my cycle, I did not get into Spelman, my first choice. I wanted to get out of Florida, and Howard was just too big, too far, and too cold. I decided to attend Clark Atlanta. I figured I should major in mass communications, go back to Miami, and get hired right away because of my relationships and experience in the field. This was what I thought I needed to do. It was my mindset at the time. This job would pay my bills and give me the freedom I wanted to be a grownup.

I graduated from high school and went off to college. Spelman, Morehouse, Clark Atlanta, Morris Brown, and the Interdenominational Theological Center are the five colleges and universities that make up the Atlanta University Center. I had two friends from high school who attended Morehouse College, so I wasn't alone. These five colleges were all within walking distance of one another. You have the ability to feel like you are on a large university campus while experiencing the small and intimate college setting feel. I think it's a great place for students who want a Historically Black College experience.

Each school has its own personality. When I was there, Spelman was the intimate, nurturing, yet academically challenging institution for women only. Morehouse was the all-male institution that was competitive yet uplifting for black men. Clark Atlanta had the big, social school feel with a football team and fraternity and sorority life. Morris Brown was the nurturing family environment where students could go when they needed an opportunity. Each of these schools has contributed much to the legacy of African American brilliance in our country. For someone like me, who wanted to get away from all the stereotypes of Miami, the AUC and being in Atlanta were an incredible exposure of what life had to offer. It was my freshman year when I started realizing that there had to be more to life than just having a job and working to pay bills every day.

I was earning good grades, adjusting well to being on my own, and I began to understand what I wanted for myself and for my life.

Attending CAU was an important chapter in my life. I made friends, enjoyed the social events, and had my first taste of music outside of Miami.

I started taking some of my classes to prepare for my major and, at the same time, cross-registered and took a tap class at Spelman. When I walked on that campus, I still felt like that was where I needed to be. There was a yearning inside of me that said I needed to be a in a smaller, more concentrated place where I would learn more about myself. I also knew that the major I'd chosen in communications just wasn't my passion. I learned then the importance of majoring in the subject(s) that you are passionate about. I researched what I would major in at Spelman and pictured myself there. I reapplied to Spelman and, this time, I got in. Apparently, this pattern of not making it the first time was something that was going to continue to show up in my life.

When I arrived at Spelman, I had to adjust to coming in as a transfer, but I finally felt at home. I remained involved with NAACP and became the college chapter president. I decided to double-major in both sociology and drama. I learned that majoring in communications was a way of making a living, but it wasn't making the life I wanted, nor would it make me feel fulfilled. I have to say that it was a blessing to learn that lesson so early in life.

I often get the chance to speak to groups in Georgia and around the country, and it's advice that I give to college and high school students all the time. They sometimes get caught up in what their parents think they should major in, what comes easy to them, or even what will make them the most money. Think about people you know who simply exist and work to pay bills. They don't enjoy life, they don't enjoy their work, and, therefore, they probably are unfulfilled. I can't imagine living a life that is just good enough to get by, or even working in a field that doesn't inspire me to want to get up in the morning.

My double major allowed me to work on the two things I loved the most. Being at Spelman was a life-changing experience. It opened up my whole world as I learned about myself as a black woman, had opportunities to perform in productions, worked on issues through the NAACP, and even created a theater program called the Niamani project that empowered kids to express themselves about pressing social issues through the arts.

One of my most memorable experiences in college was organizing students around the issue of Affirmative Action. There was a legislator with a bill that would dismantle Affirmative Action programs in Georgia. We immediately joined forces with other groups around the Atlanta area. We participated in a march to the state capitol. It was unimaginable how cold it was that day in January. It was raining and freezing. I remember the late Earl T. Shinhoster, who was the Southeast Regional Director of the NAACP at the time and one of my mentors; he was a part of the march, too. He loaned me his hat to cover my head from the rain, and someone else loaned me their gloves.

I remember getting back to campus and discovering that I had frostbite for the first time. More than the cold and the frostbite, I remembered what it felt like to be a part of something that was bigger than me. We believed that Representative Earl Ehrhart, whose bill it was to destroy Affirmative Action, was wrong; and we weren't going to stand around and watch opportunities for students of color and minority businesses get snatched away. The bill died in committee by one vote. We believe that our efforts—letter-writing and participating in the process—made a difference. When I was marching as a student and standing up for what I believed in, I would have no idea that just four years later I would be serving from the same county as Earl Ehrhart, nor that I would be one of those legislators who would one day be lobbied by some of these same groups.

As a result of my involvement with the march and serving as president of the Spelman NAACP chapter, I became involved with the Georgia Coalition for the People's Agenda. That's where I met the person who would have the biggest impact on my philosophy of public service and leadership style: Dr. Joseph Echols Lowery. It's through my involvement in the People's Agenda that I became more aware of, not only the work of Dr. Lowery, but also his heart. I have learned much from him, through the wisdom and history that he shares in those meetings and through his actions. I have watched him week by week, day by day, operating with the utmost integrity and heart for the people. I have yet to meet another person who can literally walk with the royalty of other nations or United States presidents and place their same value on someone with no title at all.

Dr. Lowery has lived his entire life standing up for other people. He's been a pastor and president of the Southern Christian Leadership Conference for over twenty years; and now, at eighty-eight years old, he continues to wake up every single day, working to help other people. He doesn't complain. It seems his fire never dies, and he consistently speaks up for the least of these without ever changing who he is or the words he chooses (you can do that at eighty-eight), or apologizing for it. I've learned so much about what servant leadership is from Dr. Lowery, and no one makes me feel more honored to know them and call them friend or mentor.

Dr. Lowery calls me one of his daughters and nicknamed me "Youngblood." His example often helps me make decisions on where and how I will stand on issues in the legislature. When I'm faced with a tough decision or need some advice, I often call Dr. Lowery. That's because I know there is no question of agendas or personal benefits. It doesn't mean that we agree on every issue (school choice is one of them), but when it comes to the issues, I can count on Dr. Lowery to always stand on the side where the masses will benefit. I've seen him give up his own money and honorariums for speaking engagements (he can electrify any crowd with his soul-stirring speeches) for the good of the People's Agenda or the institute created in his name. I serve on both boards for those organizations. I have watched him and seen, time and time again, his unwavering commitment to justice and equality for all people and the personal sacrifices he makes to leave this world a better place than he found it.

I graduated from Spelman in 2000, a much stronger, more passionate woman, ready to put my newly discovered purpose, developed skills, and degree to work. I took my first job with a national organization based in Washington, D.C. In that capacity, I would find myself back at the capitol, not just in Georgia, but in other states around the Southeast. I was training young people to lobby on gun violence issues. The skills I was developing while teaching them would plant seeds in my spirit about public service and having a seat at the table. All of the experiences in the NAACP, organizing at Spelman, my involvement with the People's Agenda, and my new job would all be great preparation for the next steps in my life that would lead me to public service.

As I look back now, I can see why some of my teachers in high school and friends in college aren't surprised that I'm an elected official. I was an organizer at heart and didn't know it. Whether it was my failed attempt to start an African American heritage club that put me in front of the school board in Miami; the early exposure to the political process in high school and college; the march to the state capitol in Georgia; or my job empowering young people to change the laws on the accessibility of firearms in their community—I was being prepared for a life in public service.

❧ LESSONS I LEARNED ALONG THE WAY ❧

1. **Never apologize for following your passion.** Sometimes what's comfortable is not always the route you should take. Watch the people in your life who are most at peace and fulfilled in their lives. These are the people who are following their passions. Fear is often what keeps us away from the life we want, and then we end up settling for the life we have. Shouldn't we change the way we look at life? Shouldn't we all have the opportunity to wake up in the morning looking forward to the work we have to do? Follow your passion and live on *purpose.*

2. **Don't give up when you are let down.** Sometimes life doesn't happen the way we've planned. When it doesn't happen that way, we immediately begin to question ourselves, our abilities, and sometimes our own purpose. Understand that life doesn't always happen on your timeline. Just because you didn't get something the first time doesn't mean it's not for you. Don't be so quick to give up on a dream because it didn't happen the way *you* thought it would happen.

3. **Appreciate the lessons on your detour.** Have you ever started out with one goal, but, along the way, you ended up on another path and appreciated the things you saw there? Whether you stayed on that path or not, you realized that if you had continued on the original journey you wouldn't have appreciated the destination as much. We have to open ourselves to what life and God want to teach us.

The year I didn't get into Spelman and attended CAU first, I learned one of the most important lessons in life. This was the importance of doing what you are passionate about. It's the best advice I can give to high school or college students—and even people who are unhappy in their present situation in life. If I had spent the entire year moping about not being accepted to Spelman, or perhaps had even gone to Spelman first as originally planned—I may not have learned that most powerful lesson. Take the time to learn, explore, and take in all that this detour on your path has to offer.

4. Give the gift of exposure. Just because you are in a certain place in your life doesn't always mean that's where you are supposed to stay. Getting out and exposing yourself to different places, ideas, things, and people allow you to explore what life has to offer. Sometimes we can get stuck in what we know and what surrounds us. Open yourself to new things and give yourself, and your children, more of what life has to offer. Exposure helps us to dream beyond the moment and present circumstances. It inspires us to want more for ourselves, to learn new things, and even to discover a new passion.

3. THERE'S NO SUCH THING AS BALANCE

IN JANUARY OF 2002, RIGHT before I was to announce my run for the state house, I met my husband David. We were connected by a mutual friend to work on a project David was trying to organize for his nonprofit. I was always attracted to guys who were passionate about the community. David was one of those guys.

When David walked up to my glass office door, I had to take a second look. I remember everything about that day. He was dressed in a button-down shirt and tie looking like the ultimate Alpha man. Greek-lettered organizations are a huge part of life when you attend a Historically Black College or University. Many of us were first introduced to fraternities and sororities from the movie *School Daze*. After watching it, many of us wanted to wear those sweatshirts or jackets and step on campus. I knew that when I got to college I wanted to be an "AKA" (a member of Alpha Kappa Alpha Sorority, Incorporated). I didn't get the opportunity to "pledge" at Spelman, but I was still determined to become a member of the nation's oldest African American female sorority. Eventually, after college, I did.

All through college, I was attracted to Alpha men. There was something about those well-dressed, intelligent brothers of Alpha that caught my eye. I used to envision driving my car with my Alpha/AKA tag, riding to my house in my nice subdivision with my 2.5 kids and cat. David is intelligent, an Alpha, and a fine brother. He always squirms when I say things like that, but it's the truth. According to him, he doesn't have the same recollections about our meeting, because he was trying to "handle his business." It must have been a lot of business, because our meeting lasted three hours that day.

We talked about everything under the sun; he has the type of personality that makes anyone feel extremely comfortable around him. We quickly began to talk on a regular basis, enjoying each other's company, inspired by each other's goals. We started dating a month to the day after we met. That was about two months before I announced my candidacy.

Although he doesn't remember (conveniently), he wasn't exactly my star volunteer on the campaign at first. My friends who worked on the first campaign remember pretty well how we would all be out campaigning, knocking on doors, putting out flyers, or phone banking every day. We would come back to headquarters—the house I'd bought when I was twenty-one—and David would be sitting on the couch watching both the television and the people going through the house.

After a while, he began to get used to the idea of the campaign, and he eventually became of one my major motivators and a key volunteer. He caught the campaign fever and would have to get me out of bed those early mornings to go and wave to rush hour traffic. He was my constant reminder that I had to stay the course and get up, even when I didn't feel like it. That was one of the things that attracted me to him. I discovered I needed a partner in life who would push me and hold me accountable. Some of us need that more than others. Some of us don't like being held accountable, but I don't mind it, as long as it's someone I *want* to hold me accountable. David and I do that for each other.

I was elected in November 2002, and we married in 2003. We had a beautiful wedding in Cobb County, surrounded by our loved ones and friends. The lead-up to the wedding wasn't so much fun. Because of my bout with the Sons of Confederate Veterans (which I will talk about in a later chapter), they threatened to protest at my wedding. While I was concerned about my "something borrowed and something blue," I was also concerned about any uninvited guests that wanted to crash my wedding. Thank God, they at least had enough class not to show, and the wedding went off without a hitch.

Our first couple of years of marriage were filled with the same ups and downs as every other marriage. We had to figure out how to communicate with one another, which habits annoyed each other, and how to compromise. By the third year of our marriage, David had inherited a principal position at a charter school that was quickly going downhill. From what I saw, the school board in that area was doing all that it could to starve it of funds, and David had neither the skill sets he needed to handle such a crisis, nor the support of colleagues around him.

At one point, he was working fifteen-hour days, not sleeping at night, and not getting paid. He was under so much stress from it all—using his own money to meet payroll and carrying so much weight on his shoulders—that he would sometimes jump up in the middle of his sleep or not sleep at all. He went to work every day, not knowing who was going to quit, who was conspiring against him, or whether the heat would work in the dead of winter. It was a tremendous burden to carry, and I have no doubt that he was trying to carry it alone.

Coincidently, we had spent that entire year trying to get pregnant. Two years into our marriage, we started planning for a family, but clearly God had another plan. We tried for months. I read all of the books; I tried all of the home remedies. Nothing was happening. I was surrounded by close friends who had beautiful babies, and I could only watch them as they seemed to enjoy the part of their lives that we had all dreamed about and planned for as we were growing up.

I went back and forth to the doctor and discovered I have PCOS. This is a disorder that is much more common among women than we realize, one that causes cysts to grow on our ovaries. It is a form of infertility that can be treated with surgery or medicine to shrink the cysts. It wasn't until I was diagnosed with it that my mother finally admitted that she had it as well. It turned out that she, too, had had problems getting pregnant until she had the surgery. She was afraid that she was the reason and blamed herself.

Medical advances are such that surgery wasn't necessary. I started taking a prescribed medicine twice a day and continued all of the other methods. I even had David get tested to make sure he wasn't the problem. He was patient and cooperative as we struggled through this process. I wanted to be a mother so badly. Something like this consumes so much of what you do and think when things don't work out the way you planned. David was incredibly supportive. He would always tell me to have faith. While in our bedroom, he would remind me that one day I would be changing our baby's diaper on the side of the bed. I kept envisioning that picture and held on to it to get through what seemed like a lifetime of waiting.

We even went to a fertility doctor, because I was impatient in this process. It had been almost a year, and I didn't understand why it was taking so long. I trusted David, and, of course, I trusted God, but I wanted to see what advanced medicine could do to help. On the first visit, I was tested for everything under the sun. The doctor conducted at least twenty different tests with my blood to find the reason I had not gotten pregnant. They also took a pregnancy test. I laughed at that one because that was the reason I was there in the first place.

I had to go back the second day to complete a test and get some of my results. David had to go to work, so I went by myself. As I was sitting in the chair getting counseled on a new medicine I was to start, the nurse opened my folder and her eyes bulged. She smiled, and then looked again. She went over to her computer to look something up, then looked at me. She said, "Mrs. Morgan, you're pregnant!" Needless to say, I was in total disbelief, so much so that I left the office and went to the store to buy a pregnancy test. Despite the determination of a medically trained expert at the doctor's office, I didn't believe it until I saw the plus sign in the pregnancy test. I got back home, and David was there ironing. I had called before I got home to make sure he was there. There was no way I could give him this news over the phone or wait until he got home later that night. As he was ironing, I told him to brace himself, and I gave him the news. We were having a baby. That was absolutely one of the most exhilarating days of my life. I saw faith come to fruition.

As soon as we got pregnant, it seemed as if the issues at David's school got worse by the day. The pregnancy I had imagined—where my husband would dote over me and this life growing inside of me—went largely ignored, because he was too wrapped up in his life at the school. Even after Lailah was born, the school saga continued. He tried to be present for Lailah, but he couldn't provide for her or our family during that time. Being able to provide is wrapped up in how David and many men define their manhood. I think he felt powerless and out of control in every aspect of his life.

Eventually, the school closed, as did nearly our marriage. David became increasingly introverted and—I would say—angry with himself. He had always had an anger issue, which would take our arguments to the edge most days. At that point, it was out of control, and I had seen enough of that growing up to know that I was not going to live like that or subject my daughter to it. Admittedly, my tongue never helped the situation, because I was quick to make a snide comment or remind him of his shortcomings. Most people had no idea of what I was dealing with at home.

This is one of the challenges you face when in public life. Sometimes your pain has to be hidden to ensure that your personal life isn't exploited. I started going to individual counseling, because I was questioning myself, my judgment, and my life; I went because I felt like I was working to empower other people through my work, yet felt disempowered over my entire life at home. Those issues I faced at home and in my marriage were permeating other aspects of my life, and I knew I needed to get myself centered.

Not only did I go to individual counseling; David and I attempted marital counseling as well. For some reason it's taboo in many communities, but I'm not sure why. While we tried to work out the issues for the sake of our marriage and the commitments we had made to one another, I had to figure out what was going on with me as well. I needed somewhere that I could go where my title didn't matter and I could talk about what was going on in my head and heart. I needed to bounce some things off of someone who would be unbiased, could offer a professional opinion, and would hold me accountable. I could have gone and talked to my mother, with whom I am very close, or even some of my friends; but I also had to have the space to say out loud some of the things that scared even me. I needed someone who could guide me through a process to really figure things out in my life.

I wanted to get back to a place where the speeches I was giving lined up with what I was living in my own life. I was encouraging people to be empowered and to have the courage to make life decisions that were sometimes uncomfortable, and I needed to live what I was telling other people to do. Therapy helped me through that process of making tough decisions about my well-being and my marriage. We all have to do that for ourselves, for the sake of our sanity and mental health. We have to let go of the judgment and give ourselves the space to get professional guidance that will help us with the tough times and unanswered life questions. I'm so glad I made that decision.

Things got so bad in our marriage that David and I agreed to separate. He had totally withdrawn from his family, and I felt like he was a stranger in our home. The man who once took pride in providing for his family was no longer mentally, financially, or emotionally present. I knew we couldn't function like this. Telling him we needed to separate was one of the hardest decisions that I had to make, and was equally hard for him to accept. We separated the weekend after Thanksgiving that year. Most people didn't know, including most members of our families and even our neighbors.

It was a difficult six months of readjustment for both of us. It was difficult to subject our daughter to going back and forth between us to ensure that we both spent time with her. It was critical, though, to heal and fix what was going on with both of us. I went through meetings and an entire legislative session with people asking about my husband. I would simply reply that he was doing fine, and move on. I wasn't sure what the end result would be, but I always held onto hope that, one day, I would have back the man I first fell in love with. In no way am I suggesting that there was nothing for me to work on, but even David would say that a lot was happening with him, and separating was the best thing we could have done.

During that time, David also went through anger management classes. It was something I had always wanted him to do. I had even promised myself early in our relationship he would have to go through them before we went any further, but I always gave in and hoped that someday his anger issues would get better. I hadn't wanted to let go of our marriage and the sporadic moments of happiness. I realize now what a big mistake it was for me not to stand up for myself early on. During our separation, I finally gathered the courage to put my foot down for *me* and to not even consider reconciliation until he completed the twelve-week course.

Being separated from my husband and living as a single parent was taxing at best. I am sure that people would have advised me to let him stay and work it out. Some prefer the approach of living together while working it out. I do to, too, when the conditions in the home are conducive to that. I absolutely make no apologies for my decision, and I certainly have no regrets. I made it a nonnegotiable when I was growing up and came into my own as an adult; I was going to break the cycle of unhealthy marriage, verbal and physical abuse, and failed attempts to thrive in an unhappy situation. Life is too precious to live it in misery.

As important as it was to my own mental health and happiness, I was also not going to subject my precious daughter to grow up observing the times my husband would ignore me for days or not display any type of affection. I wanted my daughter to see parents who loved her—and one another. I wanted her to see an example of what a healthy marriage looks like. I was committed to having all of those things with David, but not from a place without love. Too many of us are willing to accept unhealthy and abusive marriages, because we don't want to be embarrassed; we feel like we have failed, or, worse, we believe we don't deserve any better. Marriage is the most personal and intimate relationship we will have. We have to work to achieve healthy marriages that help us grow and become better, not diminish who we are and what we are called to do in our lives. This doesn't mean to run out and get a divorce the moment trouble arises. It means to create some boundaries, to work within them to achieve the marriage you both want, and, yes, to make no apologies for it.

It was the absolute best thing that could have happened, because those classes have completely changed David and made him an even better man. I'm proud of him for acknowledging his need and voluntarily attending three months of classes where everyone else was forced to go by court order. It takes a real man to take that kind of step for himself. It caused me to love and respect David even more.

Marriage is challenging, especially if you strive to have a fulfilling marriage. It's even more difficult when you add the dynamic of reverse gender roles. We've never had the conversation, but I'm positive that being a public figure affects my marriage. In traditional situations, the man is the elected official, and the woman is the wife who simply takes care of all of his affairs. When you are carrying the load of being a black man in America, on top of being a man married to the public figure, I think you have to be stronger than the average man and quite comfortable in your manhood. I know it was difficult for David to come home from a challenging day at work with the walls closing in on him, and not being able to get a home-cooked meal because his wife was out at a public meeting. I saw it come up in arguments. It caused me to play down my accomplishments, because I felt I was married to a man who wasn't comfortable with himself or the cards life had dealt him at that time.

The more I talk to elected women, the more I realize what a real issue achieving healthy personal relationships is for women in the public eye. It crosses racial lines, too. I am also starting to see that it affects not only elected women, but women who are in the public eye in general.

Some of the more seasoned women seem to have experiences on both extremes. I have colleagues who have been divorced once or twice, because they've found it difficult to maintain those marriages and serve in public eye. I have also had one colleague strongly encourage me to essentially diminish myself and to stay in the background when around my husband. It's painful to see women, who are simply walking in their purpose, struggle in their own homes, because the person who is supposed to love and support them is too busy licking his own wounds of inadequacy.

This issue has become a part of my discussion with women who want to run for office. It's critical to choose partners who will support all aspects of who you are and what comes with being in the public eye, not just your role at home. Significant others have to understand, up front, that people will come over to your table at a restaurant to talk to you about an issue or to tell you how much they appreciate your work. People will tell your significant other how lucky he is to have you, and that significant other should be able to genuinely agree with them. I encourage women who are thinking about running for office to really think about the impact on their partner and where they are in their own lives.

I've found that partners who aren't comfortable in their own skin can't be the kind of partner needed by women like me. This issue has to be a part of the decision-making process when women are dating and choosing their mates. Is this is a person who can handle being in the limelight? Can he handle people watching what he does in public? It's a tough reality, but it comes along with the territory of being in the public eye. There are events and receptions I want my husband to go to. If it's important to you that your partner can carry himself well at a networking event or a reception, you have to consider that when making a relationship decision.

If your partner can't celebrate your accomplishments and be proud of who you are, how can he really support your work and encourage you in those difficult moments? Men serving in public office probably don't have to think about this, but I've found it's a real challenge for women. In fact, my female colleagues in the legislature often joke that we wish we had wives—someone who can help with the day-to-day operations, cook and clean, take care of all the responsibilities while we go out and serve the people. It's funny but true.

I rarely accept that women have it harder than men. I reject that, in life, women have to work harder, act like a man, or do any of those other things that I hear women say we must do in order for us to be equal to men. I do believe that, in the case of being in the public eye, women do have to consider things that men don't. While women are typically the spouse and support for their men, in our world, it's the other way around. Women like me have to choose men who are man enough to handle all that comes with being with us. Once you find such a person, it's a blessing. In a world where we have to be "on," it's critical to be able to come home to a person who appreciates the work you do for others *and* loves you just for who you are. It's what we need, and it's what each one of us deserves.

During the most difficult times in our marriage, I couldn't count on my husband to be there for me, and he wouldn't let me be there for him. Over that six-month period of separation, I watched my husband struggle with his selfhood and try to find a way to provide for his newborn daughter and his then twelve-year-old son, all while living with his parents again. I watched him struggle to pay for anger management courses while he toiled over his next steps. I watched him rebuild his life over that period, and I finally began to see again the man I fell in love with.

When he finished his twelve-week anger management course, I saw a man who could now control his emotions. I saw him support his children, both financially and emotionally, and felt his love toward me again. Eventually, we reunited and agreed that the separation had been important for us to do. It's a complete turnaround now, as he was recently elected to our local school board and is now doing work that he is passionate about. He's fulfilled in his own life again. He's providing, he's loving, and he clearly feels like a man again. I can't remember the last time I bought a diaper, milk, or even toiletries for our household, because my husband does all he can to take care of our family.

While I didn't, at first, love the idea of David running for the school board so soon after our separation, I appreciate my pastor, Wilbur Purvis III, for encouraging me to support David. Pastor knew that David getting elected would help our marriage. He was so right. David better understands public life, being in the limelight, and wanting a supportive spouse; and, in me, he has a partner with whom he can share his frustrations and triumphs in public service. I think it's helped our marriage by leaps and bounds. His anger management and getting back on his feet, coupled with being in public office himself, has done wonders for our marriage. I'm proud of the work that he is doing in education, and it's even brought us closer, since we can now work on an issue together—he on the local level, me on the state. No marriage is perfect, but we continue to work at it and enjoy each other's company again.

David is my life partner, and he challenges me and gives me great advice because he knows me and believes in me. I know I do the same for him. We spend a lot of time trying to create the marriage that we both want. I've learned that, despite the lack of good examples, the possibilities are limitless for having the kind of marriage two people want. When something doesn't work, you just try something else. You keep trying, because, as long as you have chosen the right partner, divorce is not an option. You can't give up when the going gets tough or when you don't feel the excitement you used to feel. Instead you work together and find a way to get where you want to be.

My whole separation experience has also taught me not to be silent about how hard it is to be a wife. It took a lot for me to share that very recent experience in my marriage. I realized, though, that if I am to encourage people to talk more about the realities of their lives, I would have to open up and share, too. I've learned over the years that we have to do more of that. David and I both believe in the importance of couples linking up to talk about marriage and share best practices. It was one of my good friends who summed it up like this: men want to be respected and women want to be loved. That rings so true in my marriage. I wonder how much strife we could have avoided if we had really understood those needs years ago. But I wouldn't have known that principle if my friend and I hadn't been sharing with one another the real difficulties of marriage.

It seems like marriage is different today, not just because the statistics for divorce are so much higher, but because, I think, our generation sees marriage differently. It's not necessarily that we don't value it as much. I think we just aren't willing to accept less. How many of us have parents whose marriage is more about what's comfortable rather than what's healthy? When I hear about couples who have been married a long time, I always wonder if they are actually happy or just surviving. I can't imagine being in a relationship and just surviving. We also can't base our relationships and the terms of our marriages on someone else's relationship or what was typical thirty years ago. We have to renegotiate those terms for ourselves and determine what fulfills and works for us. It may be different for each couple, but we have the opportunity to create the marriages that we want. The sky is the limit.

So, how do I serve in elected office, hold down more than one job, and maintain a family? One of the biggest challenges that the twenty-first-century woman faces today is so-called "work life balance." Gone are the days when women like me were satisfied or fulfilled with solely being at home caring for the children and the household. Obviously, there are plenty of women who do that and enjoy it. I say more power to them. I honor them and appreciate them for having that as their passion. Women are now in a place to choose their life work, and my position is: as long as *she* chooses to work or to stay at home, then society should let her be. We should let women decide if they want to work and/or have a family.

Although times have changed, many of us still have that old-school mindset; some would even call it internalized sexism that says that women should choose a families first, careers second, and then everything else. We can all get caught up in what we think are society's "norms." I even find myself looking with great admiration at other moms who dedicate their entire lives to their children, and saying to myself, "I wish I could do that." In no way does it make me want to change my life or who I am, but the world has taught women that we should question ourselves and one another when there seems to be a choice of one over the other.

Let me define what I mean when I talk about work, family, and personal life. I don't list these in a particular order, but, too often, women feel the pressure of having to choose. What I know about life is that it's important to allow yourself to be comfortable in decisions you make about your life and what's most important for you at the time, rather than to be swept up in what society, your friend, or your mother says.

I contribute to my family as a wife and a mother, and I also contribute to the running of our household by working and helping to provide for our family. I've always been given the advice from other women to make sure that, no matter what my family situation is, I always have a way to provide for myself so that I am never solely dependent upon any other person. For me, I choose to work, because I am walking in my purpose; it also puts me in a position to take care of myself and my family in the event of an emergency or my husband's inability to provide.

Working also gives me the feeling of contributing to something outside of myself. It also gives me the power to make financial decisions with a sense of freedom. For women who choose otherwise, they have to be comfortable in that decision, but I have to say I think it's a fine line when a woman allows herself to be in a position where she is solely dependent on another person for her financial well-being. I think it's completely possible to allow your mate to take care of the household, while always being in a position to step in and take care of yourself, should the need arise.

Women who choose to work sometimes feel the tug-of-war between work and family. Families of today are different from past families as well. Not everyone subscribes to the husband and wife, two kids, and a dog that barks. For some, family is a spouse; for others it's kids with no spouse. While we try to create a schedule that allows us to contribute to the working world, we often feel the strain of spending time with family to ensure their growth and development, and to meet all of their social, emotional, and physical needs. We don't want to work so much and climb the ladder of success so fast that our kids don't know who we are,—nor do we know them. We want to create those family moments that we will cherish for life. I remember our family vacations, the long rides and van that smelled like my dad's famous ribs. I don't want to get so caught up in working that I forget about the people at home or the responsibility I have to meet their needs.

In the midst of working and raising a family, so many couples forget about maintaining their own relationships. Somehow, we think we should be fulfilled in our marriage by spending time with the entire family, including the children (if there are children). It inevitably means that your focus is on other family members and not your partner. So many of us did not have strong models of this growing up, and, in our adult lives, we continue to try to figure out how to do something that we have never seen ourselves—present company included.

To have a strong marriage or relationship with our significant other, we have to create space for that relationship as well. I don't mean meeting time to discuss bills, the children, or our jobs; I mean real time to laugh and enjoy each other's company. I mean being deliberate about setting time to spend together: special occasions, date nights, and time to forget about responsibilities and remember why you fell in love in the first place. Carving out that time and being deliberate about it helps sustain the relationship and helps keep the balance we need. It's also about modeling for your children so they see love, relationship, and a connection beyond the family unit. David and I have gotten much better about this as we have weekly lunches, monthly bubble baths, and try to get together with other couples for double dates as often as we can.

In the midst of being a loving wife, nurturing mother, and public servant (not always in that order or at the level I would like), I know that I also have to do things for me. Women have to do things for enjoyment or enrichment, and to create a more well-rounded life for themselves. Whether that means hanging out with your girlfriends, going to plays with your mom, or gardening, it's something that no one is forcing you to do—you've carved out time and space to accommodate it, and your benefit is not monetary.

This is the area for women that usually requires the most help. Women tend to make this third on the list of priorities or the item that gets left undone. I wish we would figure out that having a healthy personal life makes us better in all of our other worlds. That concept does not transfer to other areas. Making more time for work does not make you a better mother. Carving out more time for family does not always translate to a better employee or business owner. Spend time for yourself—whether it's reading a good book, a date night with your friends, or taking up a new hobby that takes you away from your everyday life and immerses you in an experience where you don't have to focus on your life or responsibilities.

In those moments when I feel that I'm getting overwhelmed or that my tank is empty, I try to stop and take in some "me" time. I will take a "me" day, which includes my three favorite things: eating (most likely at Red Lobster), a massage, and a little retail therapy. Everyone knows that when it's a "me" day, I'm unreachable. I know—in order to keep my sanity—I have to do it. Otherwise, I'm no good for anyone. I can't make good decisions, I can't think clearly, and I am unlikely to give my all. I've learned over the years to take better care of myself so I can take better care of all the things and people who depend on me.

Sometimes women feel like these three aspects of our lives are constantly pulling at us. We want to be the best in all areas of our lives, but we quickly find that as we focus on one thing, something else seems to suffer. The question we often ask is, how we can do it all? We ask if we can we balance those things. My answer is, no we can't, and we shouldn't even try. Balance suggests that everything gets the same amount of attention all of the time. That doesn't work, because at some point one of those pieces needs more attention than the others. If you have convinced yourself that you can balance it all when your husband needs some extra attention or your child is sick, something has to suffer at work or in your personal life. Trying to balance all that is like trying to plug the holes where water is shooting out from everywhere. As soon as you plug one or two, another hole shoots more water. Trying to fill all of those holes is exhausting to say the least, not to mention a waste of energy.

One of my good friends in public service, Lisa Borders, who is the former president of the Atlanta City Council, said it best. Women shouldn't aim to balance it all, but, instead, should be the best at what they are at the moment. She says, when you are at home being a wife or significant other, be the best at that very moment. When you are being a mom, be the best mom you can be at that very moment. When you are at work or at church—wherever you are—be the best that you can be in that moment. It's almost liberating to hear that. Rather than pressuring ourselves to be everything to everybody, just stop and be the best at what you are doing in that moment. Block out the rest of the stuff going on, and focus on being your best and doing your best for the people who need you at that moment. It's a paradigm shift. It's a notion that challenges everything we thought we had to do, but it really helps us to put things in perspective. I couldn't have verbalized that better, so I thank Lisa for sharing that with me and a group of young, elected women we hosted for a conference recently.

It's time for us to start rejecting the models that people and society have said we should fit. There is not a one-size-fits-all model that fits each of our needs. We are uniquely made and have the right to operate in what works best for us. We should acknowledge those things that really are first priority in our lives. For some women, career is the most important thing; therefore, they choose to delay getting married or having children. When we see women who have been married or committed for a while, we start to wonder as a society when the baby is coming, or we ask why they aren't married. We have a hard time believing that there are women who want to delay childbearing or choose not to have children at all. Why? Because all of our lives, girls and women are groomed to look forward to motherhood. We're given dolls to play with and to teach, and we learn from our mothers how to mother. We are naturally nurturers, so why not look forward to doing for our own children what our mothers did for us?

Despite my own successes in life, why wouldn't I look at a stay-at-home mom with envy when society tells us that motherhood is our greatest accomplishment? It's what we believe we are supposed to do, which is why, as a society, we are puzzled by women who choose not to have children or have them later in life. As a result, I think some women put all of their energy into their children without carving a space for their own interests. Those who really want to work and contribute in other ways find themselves resentful of their husbands, their friends, and of life, because they have given up their own dreams to live someone else's. Again, to those women whose choice it is to stay at home, those who find their joy in raising children, I say, congratulations. For those women who are making that choice over their own heart's desires, we need to free them of our judgment and empower them to live the life they were called to live.

Some women decide they want to focus on their careers before they get married or have children. Some simply want a career without a family. Sadly, we judge them for that. We start questioning their judgment, their moral compass, or wonder about their sexuality. Does there have to be something "wrong" with a woman who chooses career over family? I say, absolutely not. In fact, shouldn't we applaud a woman who acknowledges her strengths and priorities? Wouldn't so many children be better off if their mothers had recognized their real priorities rather than succumb to the pressures of their families or the ladies in church who ask when the babies are coming?

There are women who have decided that they want both the family and the career. I'm that kind of woman. Family is key to me, and, yes, for me, family comes first. For me, it means that there are times when my schedule requires me to travel, to be in meetings all day, and to miss the occasional meeting or basketball game at my stepson's school. It also means that there are days when I say no to my professional obligations, because that day is set aside for my family or myself. It doesn't matter who's making the request or how important the meeting is; I have set my boundaries, and, for that designated time, I am not available.

Wherever I am, I am working on being the best me in that moment. Most evenings, when session is in or I'm working on a project, I could be away from home five evenings out of the week. That doesn't mean that the next week I will make sure that I'm home five days to make up for the week before. It does mean that, during the moments I have with my family, we are together and we are working to make those moments count. It means being deliberate about scheduling time together and checking in with my husband and kids to make sure they are okay. It means acknowledging my absence, being sensitive to accepting or denying requests on my schedule, and trying my best to be completely present for the people I love. For some, that's difficult. I know others question how I can be a good wife or mother with all of my other obligations. I make no apologies for it, because I know this is the life my husband and I have both chosen; I thank God we have the support of family around us to make it work.

Young women often ask how I balance having a small child with my schedule. The answers are simple. First, I challenge them to let themselves off the hook from balance. I explain that I have a husband who is also a great father. I'm not sure how common that is. I often hear older women talk about the absence of their husbands during child rearing. In my own early experience, that was the case.

My father worked three jobs at a time while I was growing up, and that required him to be gone seven days a week. My mother had to take on working two jobs and being a mother. When I hear women talk about the absence of their husbands, I hear resentment in their voices. I sense the frustration they felt. I remember when I was pregnant; friends in my own age group warned that once I had my baby it would be my baby alone. They warned that I would be the one most responsible for most things, and Daddy would be there to "babysit" when he was available. Thank God, that is not my situation.

Women who do choose both family and a career should be very careful about the mates they choose. Having a mate who does more than "help" is critical to achieving the so-called "balance" of work and family. I can't pretend that I had much insight at twenty-five when I got married, but I did have enough insight to know—from the way my husband dealt with his son—that he wanted to be an involved parent and that he was a great father. I believed that would translate to our daughter, and, thank God, I was right. It is critical to have a supportive spouse who appreciates what you contribute to the household financially, one who also helps with the many responsibilities that come along.

Family support is also ideal when you have a spouse, career, and children. With my schedule—and, many times, my husband's schedule—we aren't at home every evening, and we have obligations on the weekends, too. My parents live close by, and his parents live about thirty minutes away from us. Because of their proximity (and because they are great grandparents), my parents have taken on the role as co-parents. I have to be comfortable, when I am traveling or away all day, that my daughter will be well taken care of. With the support system that's around me—my husband and my parents—I can handle the business at hand without worrying about my daughter. I know that she's in a safe place with people who adore her. I also prepare myself for the un-spoiling—but that's the tradeoff. This is what works for us. I have to say, it's quite a blessing, and I wish every family had this kind of support network.

When Lailah was born, I realized for the first time that motherhood is a calling. I also learned that it is not necessarily my calling. This doesn't mean I don't love my daughter or that I'm not a good mother. It just means that motherhood alone is not my passion or my purpose. I look back and smile now about the whole experience. All my life, I looked forward to having my "American Dream" life. I would be married, have my two or three children, and live happily ever after.

Leading up to Lailah's due date, I was scared about delivery. I had to keep reminding myself about the millions of women who gave birth before me, that if they could do it successfully, so could I. I imagined what the day would be like when she was born. I thought about all of the romanticized childbirth stories of women who instantly fell in love with their babies the moment they held them in their arms. There was one big difference for me. I was under local anesthesia because I had a c-section with Lailah. I have the pictures, but I don't remember the instant love affair with Lailah because I think I was out of it.

I also recall being in the hospital and having the choice to go home. David was ready to get home, and I wanted to stay just one more day. I was frightened at the thought of having responsibility for this precious little life. There was no manual, no how-to book, no social networking site I was aware of that would lead me through each step. That moment of changing Lailah on the side of the bed had arrived, and I wasn't ready. David convinced me to go home, and he went back to work.

The first day I was alone with Lailah, I cried. I later found out it wasn't just fear; I had the "baby blues." It was the normal post-partum depression women get after childbirth. After being home for the first week, I developed high blood pressure issues. I had to go to the doctor at least once a week and had to take blood pressure medication along with the medicines I was taking for pain and healing from the c-section. For weeks, my blood pressure was high for the first time in my life. Ironically, the day I went back to work full time, my blood pressure issues went away. As beautiful, sweet, and wonderful as this bundle of joy was, and, as stressful as my public life was, working with many balls in the air, the only thing that had caused my high blood pressure was being a stay-at-home mom.

Now that I have completely scared you away from wanting to have children, I think it's important to say that this simply illustrates my point. There are women whose sole dream in life is to raise children. I think it's an amazing and miraculous thing that a person can do. I know my strengths and weaknesses. I know my purpose. I know I am a good mother to Lailah. I also know that motherhood is not my calling. Empowering people is.

I am experiencing all of the other wonderful things motherhood and having a family will do for you. The joy of watching my daughter grow up, meeting different milestones, and seeing her face light up when I enter the room are all priceless memories forever etched in my heart. To see myself in another being that I and my life partner have created is indeed incredible. It's worth all the sacrifices, juggling of schedules, and nagging from my parents about how I should do things. It's possible to have all of these things and enjoy them, but we should also be honest about how difficult all of these responsibilities can be. For David and me, we've decided that we aren't having any more children. Lailah and my stepson Rashaan are all we need. Despite having to explain this decision at least weekly, I'm comfortable with our decision, because we know the kind of life we want for ourselves and our family and make no apologies for it.

For some reason, women don't always share what's going on and the real challenges we face in being mothers, wives, and all that we are called to be in our lives. Rather than talking about the realities of what we do, or going beyond the casual "how are the kids and family" question, we smile; we pretend that everything is okay, and we hide behind the smile that is really, at times, a mask of being overwhelmed with responsibility—underappreciated and worn out. When we finally have those moments and one of us has the courage to open the door, we dump on one another with the heavy burdens we feel.

It's not that we hate our lives, don't love our spouses and children, or fail to appreciate the opportunity to work and contribute to home and society. I think it's two things: one, we are so afraid that we are failing because we don't have it together like everyone else appears to; and, two, we don't want anyone to know that we are in over our heads some days. Our moms and aunts didn't talk about it, so there must be something wrong with us. Instead, we go around smiling and carrying these burdens with a belief that everyone else is doing it well, so we dare not complain. We have to stop carrying around stresses of life that eventually affect our mental and sometimes physical health. We need not be afraid to be real with one another. No one is going to hand you a superwoman cape or an award for carrying the most stress or being overworked. No one is going to give us any extra stripes or any extra streets of gold when we get to heaven, so why do we do this to ourselves?

Much like our tendency to not talk about the stresses of life and kids, both men and women tend not to talk about the real challenges of marriage. Statistics and real life experience would tell us that most of us didn't grow up with both parents in the home. Those of us who did, didn't always have the most traditional view of what marriage is. With that, how are we then to enter in and maintain healthy marriages when we have few, if any, examples? It's easy to talk about the good old days, when divorce rates were much smaller and it seemed like life was so simple. My take is that it's a generational difference.

I consider the women in my life when I was growing up—mostly family members—who were willing to accept much more from their husbands than my friends and I will. It doesn't necessarily mean that we value marriage less; and, yes, there are some in my generation who have little to no regard for marriage. I think it means that times have changed. Some of the women who helped raise me seem more likely to accept an abusive marriage, a husband who neglects her most basic physical and emotional needs, or even a dead, but financially stable, marriage. The women I know are willing to try and work it out, but, at the signs of no change, say, "I'm out."

There is judgment on both sides. My generation judges our mothers for what we see as a lack of courage, self-esteem, or independence; our mothers see our actions as being quitters, not valuing marriage and family, or being unable to see it through. Again, we go back to the necessity of talking about these things. Our mothers tend not to share the real challenges of marriage and raising children or, more importantly, how to overcome those challenges. Men don't seem to talk at all; they just get rid of their frustration by watching sports. We don't talk inter-generationally about healthy marriages and life. Girls get the advice to keep our legs closed, not to stay out too late, to make sure the man treats us like a lady, and to make sure you have your own money. That doesn't always transfer into what to look for in a husband versus a boyfriend. That lack of communication forces too many young people to make bad decisions, and then the adults blame them for not knowing.

Marriage is a wonderful and rewarding institution when you put in the work and marry the right person. Because so many of us lack the information on how to choose the right mate beyond the degree, the paycheck, or performance in bed, we end up in situations that have gone too far to fix. Once we discover those things, we have to share them. It's when we become better as people. It's how we begin to break cycles.

❊ LESSONS I LEARNED ALONG THE WAY ❊

1. Never apologize for living the life you want. We so often get caught up in what society says we should be or how we should act. Decide what works for you and create the life that will help you reach your destiny. We are given one life, and that one belongs to you. Live it based on what you want, not what others think it should be.

2. Break the cycle. Let's stop recreating the relationships we saw growing up if they are not healthy and fulfilling. Make it a nonnegotiable in your life that you are creating healthy boundaries for yourself, and if any person wishes to be a part of your life, they have to work within the standards that will add to your life and help you get to your destination. You were destined to be great. If you allow people to come and move you away from your purpose, you are allowing them control of your life and your circumstances. Break the cycles!

3. Take time for yourself and make no apologies for it. It's past time for women to learn that they cannot take care of others if they do not take care of themselves. As much as it sounds like a cliché, it is the absolute truth. Do you remember what it was like when you were sick and could not go to work? Did the company close up shop because you were absent? Not likely. Remember that you are your most precious resource. It's great that you can work, have a family, and be a good wife, but what about you? What about the things you enjoy doing that you have put down for everyone else? Take time for yourself. Turn off the Blackberry, don't turn on the computer, and tell your boss, children, and husband that you are off for the day or the weekend.

4. Women have to learn to share with one another. Go beyond the makeup, the clothes, and swapping baby stories. Talk about the real pain and triumphs you feel in being a woman, wife, and mother. Share the best practices of how to maintain a healthy and full life, and give each other permission to just be who you are. Drop the mask and the façade we believe we have to put on because everyone else does. Let's change the way we communicate with our friends. Let's tell the truth about our relationships, our heavy loads, the challenges of motherhood, and always being "on." Let's create a space for women to get together and vent if we need to. At the same time, let's create the space to celebrate one another when things are going well. Let's share the lessons we've learned and be honest about who we really are.

5. Go to counseling. This is nothing to be ashamed of. Go and work through the issues that you have. Find a counselor or therapist you are comfortable with, and be honest with him or her and yourself. Don't allow yourself to be discouraged by the stigma. Invest in yourself and your mental health. Go because it will help you become a better you.

6. Stand up for yourself. Sometimes, for the sake of relationships, promises that we make to ourselves, or just the fear of being alone, we keep from the making the decisions to live a healthy and less stressed life. We won't take the necessary steps to create a better life for ourselves. Whatever your situation, whether it's a marriage or a friendship, do what you must do to maintain your self-worth and dignity. The people on the outside don't have to live your life—you do. Do what you need to do to live your best life. Stand up for what you know you deserve.

7. Learn to break the rules. We often think that society gets to determine how we live our lives, what's normal, and how we should operate. Let go of what "they" think you should be doing, whether it's spending a certain amount of time at work, doing certain things for your family, or making decisions based on what other people might say. Only you can live your life, and only you know your circumstances. Do those things that make you comfortable with yourself and the decisions that you make. What do you say works for you? What do you say is best for your family? That's what you should do.

4. Walking in the Dark

Whether it's learning how to navigate marriage, a new relationship, the politics at a new job, or simply starting a new chapter in life, walking in a new phase in life can be challenging and downright hard. It's why so many of us are afraid to try new things or make major changes in our lives. We don't want to walk in the unfamiliar. Even when we are in a dysfunctional situation, we sometimes stay in it because, even though we don't like it, it's what we know.

Imagine what it was like to walk into the Georgia General Assembly at twenty-three years old, two years out of college, and five years in a state I had just moved to. I remember my first day of session. There were many news stories both in television and print about the young people who were running and those of us who were successful. I felt a great deal of excitement and pressure in being the first, not really knowing what was ahead of me, but understanding that my only option was to be successful. I felt that sense of pressure, because I knew so many people around my district were excited for the first time about voting and having an elected official they could see and touch. I have a lasting impression in my mind of the older women, especially black women, who felt my election proved their work over the years was not in vain.

I also felt the pressure, perhaps unnecessarily; that I needed to prove that my win was not a fluke. According to conventional wisdom and the way the Democratic Party drew the seat, I wasn't supposed to be there. I was in a seat designed for a white man. I also knew that I was going to have to prove something about the capabilities of young people. There were plenty of others who had come to the House of Representatives in their early twenties, but I needed to prove my own point that young people needed a seat at the table as well.

On the first day of the new biennial, which is the two-year term we are elected to, all legislators take their oath. My mother held the Bible for me, and I repeated the words of my first real oath. I took it seriously and didn't want to miss the significance of that moment. Once the swearing in was over, it was down to business. We began the proceedings, and now it was time to take roll. No one had explained how the buttons worked on our desks. I didn't know to ask ahead of time. When the speaker opened the machine for us to vote present, I voted the red button while everyone else voted the green. As I struggled to undo the lonely red *N* on the voting machine, the veteran legislators laughed and enjoyed watching me sweat. The speaker locked the machine, and I will forever go down in history as voting "no" on being present my first day in office.

The rest of the session, I simply had to feel my way through. While we had orientation of the different offices that we could access for research or writing our bills, there was no structure in place to teach a new legislator how to navigate this process. I had very few people to rely on, so I had to rely on me and what came naturally. That session turned out to be a challenging one, having to deal with the Confederate flag issue. The new governor, Sonny Perdue, pulled an upset victory on the incumbent, based on two or three controversial issues, the main one being the return of the Confederate flag. This new governor could attribute a large part of his victory to the group of citizens of Georgia to whom he had promised another opportunity to regain their Confederate flag.

We wrestled in both the House and the Senate with this issue. Race became the most prevalent topic of the entire legislative session, which lasts forty days. It was by far the most divisive. Everyone stayed on their side, there was a lot of tension, and there was very little relationship-building across racial and party lines. On the day of the vote to return the Confederate flag in the battle for voters, members of the Georgia Legislative Black Caucus went up, one by one, recounting their own experiences with the Jim Crow laws and what the Confederate emblem meant to them. They talked about the separate water fountains and the way things used to be when the flag was erected in 1956. It was said that this was done during the time of an all-white legislature, said to be done to repudiate the Brown versus Board of Education decision handed down at the Supreme Court.

It was a difficult place to be; I was the only black member of the Cobb delegation and was among the minority in a majority white legislature. It seemed like race became the foundation of every discussion and thought I had that year. When the house voted to return a version of the Confederate rebel flag emblem, I felt hurt and questioned why I would have to serve in a body where both Democrats and Republicans would vote for something that was disrespectful of an entire group of citizens in our state. I found myself internalizing all that was around me and felt myself becoming an angry person inside. If only I'd had someone to talk to—someone who could help me process what was happening, to help me work through that and still get things done.

The same problem I had then, I grapple with now. It's the lack of mentors—the lack of individuals who are willing to share their knowledge. I do have people I can call on in the legislature who will give me sound advice. I didn't have someone who would take me under his or her wing and show me the ropes. Sadly, I did not see anyone I thought was a model, precisely the kind of legislator I wanted to be. I couldn't identify one legislator who could balance the ability to speak truth to power and still be effective in the legislative process. It appeared to me that doing both wasn't possible.

It seemed like the colleagues who were willing to speak up were often ostracized and disregarded, sometimes even disrespected. Their speaking-out came with severe consequences that effectively deterred other legislators from doing the same. The other legislators who seemed to be effective in terms of getting bills passed were quiet, and rarely, if ever, ruffled feathers; some had reputations for selling out to get the things they wanted. I had a difficult time working through that and continue to struggle with it even now.

One life-changing lesson I have learned throughout my time in the legislature is to choose my battles. There were times I would go to the well to speak anytime I felt strongly about something. It was my way of speaking truth to power at any given opportunity. I thought that, if my purpose was to challenge the status quo in the legislature and speak up for those who don't have a voice, I should do it every single chance I got—that was, until I started watching other legislators go and speak at every turn. I watched the eyes of my colleagues rolling; I saw how people would get up or start mumbling under their breath, "not him again." I realized the powerlessness there was in *always* having something to say.

I also realized how the same applied in my marriage and in life. We should always choose our battles. Not only does it give us a stronger voice on the issues we are deliberate in selecting, it also helps to preserve our energy for the real battles we have been called to fight. This doesn't mean that you should be completely silent. It means that maybe you can find another way to help the cause that doesn't always put you out front every time. Choosing your battles also gives you another tactic in your strategy arsenal. Those who are waiting to oppose you can no longer anticipate your every move.

The lesson of choosing my battles is one that I had to discover on my own. There are some things that your own experiences have to teach you. At times, someone telling you won't help, and sometimes there is just no one to tell you. In fact, I'm sure if someone had tried to teach me that particular lesson, I wouldn't have truly understood what they meant. Some things you just have to learn on your own. I learned that lesson after fighting so much and it only resulting in me being more angry and having fewer allies. Even in the absence of someone to show me the ropes, I did learn what I could from those I respected, even if I didn't see them entirely as the kind of legislator I wanted to be. I would then identify a particular characteristic I liked from one and pulled from that perspective. When I wanted something they didn't have, I would have to ask someone else.

I believe the strongest mentor I had during my first few years was Calvin Smyre. He has served in the legislature for more years than I have been on the earth. He is a banker and a businessman—not an activist—so his perspective is often different. He has learned a great deal throughout his tenure and has used his skills to move up through the ranks of leadership within the Democratic Caucus. He is respected in many circles and wielded a pretty heavy gavel when he served as Rules Committee Chairman. This is the committee in our legislature that determines *if,* and when, a bill will make it to the entire House for a vote. The chairman of the committee has extraordinary power to keep a bill even the governor wants from coming up for a vote. The same position exists in the Senate. What I noticed about Calvin was that he certainly played the politics, but he also tried his best to help people. He didn't mind helping members get what they needed.

Calvin is the confidant of a lot of people and holds a lot of information that people have trusted him with over the years. He tries very hard to make himself available to people who call on him, both in the legislature and out. I have no doubt that it's primarily because he understands the value of helping people and enjoys doing it. There is another part, though, that I've learned he understands—that helping is also a part of cultivating relationships, being able to call on people when you need them, and making yourself the person people call when they need help. Having that kind of personal value can help you build a great deal of power and influence; and Calvin—though he is no longer the Rules Chairman because of the Republican majority—can still utilize that power when necessary.

Calvin taught me another important lesson about politics and life. I was dealing with an issue one session, and the legislator I was working with at the time had an immense amount of influence. For an affirmative vote on his bill, this person was making offers for items in the budget. No one had ever approached me with anything like this before. I knew that how I responded would be the basis of our relationship and how I would be viewed after that. I knew I had to handle my response well. I also knew that Calvin could help me sort through the politics of this situation.

His advice was priceless. He didn't even agree with me on this issue, but he told me objectively not to make any deals, to say from the beginning where I stood on the bill and to be clear that it was not connected to anything this person could specifically do for me. He taught me that people who make those kinds of deals do two things.

First, they make a name for themselves as people who are willing to sell out and can be bought. Second, when you make that one deal, you cannot return for help on another issue in which you might be interested in the future.

After that situation was over and session had ended, I saw exactly what he was saying. Without any solicitation on my part, not only did I pass my first bill that session—something that could not have happened without the help of that legislator and the others he asked to help me—but I have a more meaningful relationship with that person. Not once did I feel like I had to compromise my values or integrity. Not once did I have to wake up and look in the mirror and be disappointed with the person looking back at me. I also saw the manifestation of what happens when you operate from your own values rather than the short-term fix you were seeking. Politics and life in general are about respect and one's own integrity. It's how you treat yourself and how you treat people when no one else is watching.

The legislators who did make specific deals with that legislator, I don't judge. I understand the desperation you feel when you want to get money in the budget, or when a bill you've been working on for years is so close to passing and making that deal solidifies it for you. I understand the real dilemma. You can go back to your district, complaining about how bad things are for Democrats (or whatever group), explaining why you can't help the school in your district buy used computers for the lab; or you can go home with a check in hand, announcing that you are building the lab and buying brand new computers.

Sometimes, the *how* is not so important to the people who are getting what they need to succeed. Instead, for many, it's about the *what* you were able to achieve for them. Most times, people don't know or care how you had to make something happen. They simply want to see it done. Most of us get elected or try to put ourselves in positions so we can help people and make life better for the masses. What we have to remind ourselves is that it's not always about the short term or about that one time. Our goal should be, first, to operate from a place of integrity and honor. Second, we should remember from our past experiences that, when we do what's right, we will be rewarded in God's time.

There are others in the legislature I call on for different things, just as there are people outside of politics on whom I call for help in my career, life decisions, and even personal relationships. Without Calvin's advice, I don't know how that situation would have turned out for me. He has given me advice on other things that I have chosen not to use because, in my gut, it didn't work for me. Of course, these are the times he complains that I "don't listen." Frankly, it's a place of real contention in our relationship.

What I know is that you take what you can from those you can learn from. When advice is given, only you know how taking it fits with the goals you've set for yourself and how they fit with your own values and beliefs. The advisor may not always agree with how you choose to use the advice, but, at the end of the day, it's you who have to make that decision. I still don't have a mentor in the legislature as I would like, but I take what I can from the different pieces I appreciate about people. The rest of the time, I know that operating from my heart and my integrity and, most importantly, in prayer, I will continue to find my own way.

Whether it's being an effective legislator or knowing how to navigate corporate America, there will be times when you feel that there is no one to turn to because no one will understand your unique situation. Other times, the people you need to talk to just aren't available for you at the time. What I learned from the experience in politics—and about life— is to always operate from your principles and values first. Everything else will eventually fall into place. During those times when I have a tough decision to make, I start with asking myself what is most important to me in this situation. What are the values here that should remain intact? How can this situation be resolved in a way that still allows me to feel good about who I am? When you ask yourself those kinds of questions, the decisions you need to make will start to fall into place.

There will be times in all of our lives when our journey takes us on a path that has never been traveled. For me, there is no one in the legislature who balances activism with effectiveness, and, therefore, *I* become that example for myself. Truthfully, I find that the circumstances in our legislature change each year; and, even if there was someone who was exactly the kind of legislator I strive to be, there are many times when no one has all of the answers or can determine how something will turn out.

For you, it could involve a business you want to create, and you know there's no one you can call on to help you figure it out. Maybe there is no book that provides you with all the steps to make it happen. Don't let that discourage you from trying. We should never be afraid of having to create our own path. Another great lesson I learned while at Clark Atlanta was the school motto, "Find a way, or make one." Take the best of all that is around you, and use your own moral compass to create the rest.

When you find yourself in a situation where there is help, don't allow pride or shame to hinder you from getting the answers you want. Having a mentor—of any kind—who can help answer questions can prevent you from making mistakes and help you get to where you want to be a lot faster. Research has shown that people with mentors tend to be more successful in their line of work. I believe that's because someone is there to help lead the way and warn you about the pitfalls before you succumb to them. Those people can also give you the heads-up on an opportunity that lies ahead because they have the ability and experience to see things you may not be able to see. If you have the opportunity to develop a relationship with a mentor or advisor, why not take advantage of that opportunity to be better at what you want? The sky is the limit, and if there is someone along the way who can help you determine how to at least get to the stars, it's time to start asking.

❖ Lessons I Learned Along the Way ❖

1. Never apologize for following your gut. Sometimes we have to make a tough decision, but the more information we get, the more confused we become. The more people who want to give you advice, the more you realize how unprepared you feel. Only you know what your gut says for you to do. Let your gut, your spirit, or that little voice inside of you help get you to the answer. Whether it yields the result you want or not, learning to trust yourself and your own principles makes you a more grounded person, one who is empowered to depend on yourself and not the agenda of other people. You have your own mind, heart, and set of life experiences, and you are equipped to make decisions that are best for you.

2. Take responsibility for what you know and what you don't know. Learn from, or accept advice from, those you trust. We don't have to know all of the answers, but we do have to acknowledge what we don't know. The wisdom to seek advice is the maturity to move through life understanding that this is a journey.

3. Choose your battles. I believe it was Tavis Smiley who said that there are some battles worth fighting, even if you never win, and other battles not worth fighting, even if you know you will win. This is a lesson we can use in the workplace, in our places of worship, and in all aspects of our lives. Think about your use of energy. Ask yourself if this battle helps you get to your ultimate goal. If it doesn't, maybe you can let that one slide or let someone else fight that battle.

4. Find mentors. We learn lessons throughout our journey—some from our failures, some from our successes. Some lessons we can learn from people who have already gone through our trials—people who can teach us about the pitfalls so that we don't have to experience them. Even if you don't have someone who does exactly what you want to do or who is taking the exact path you want to take, try to learn from people in the pieces they do have to offer; eventually those pieces can add up to a whole.

5. Don't be afraid to create your own path and walk the road less traveled. Many individuals who are record breakers and firsts in their fields accomplish their goals because they didn't let the less-worn path deter them from taking it. If you research most successful businesspeople, they will tell you about the times they failed and the times they had to learn what to do and what not to do on their own. Sometimes things were accomplished because people didn't know it was impossible. Enjoy the adventure and the excitement of un-chartered territory. Just remember, once you create the path, bring someone along after you.

Ralph Waldo Emerson once said, "Do not go where the path may lead; go instead where there is no path and leave a trail."

5. The Outsider on the Inside

THE QUESTION I'M ASKED MOST often is how I knew to run for office at twenty-two. To their surprise, it was not always in my plan. I guess that's the first lesson in all of this. Your plan may not always be the path you take at the end. I remember being in college, thinking about what I would do with my degree in sociology and drama. I knew I wanted to start a nonprofit and work with young people. This nonprofit organization would give me the space I needed to marry my two passions—the arts and empowering under-represented communities. I was going to continue the Niamani Project, the program I started while at Spelman.

Once I graduated, though, I didn't follow that path. Instead, I took a job with a national organization based in Washington, D.C. Although it was based in D.C., I stayed in Georgia. In that job, I was working with young people around the issue of gun violence. It was that job that helped me understand the legislative process and the importance of the community being involved in that process. I found myself at the Georgia state capitol, as well as other capitols in the southern region.

Of course, I didn't know it then, but that job was great preparation for what I was to do just a year later.

In 2001, I was working with some friends and community organizations to register ten thousand eighteen- to twenty-five-year-olds to vote in the municipal election that year. We called it the Atlanta 10G project. That was really the time I got to know Tharon Johnson well and first met Heather Fatzinger, who would later become one of my mentors and my campaign manager. We focused on young people because we were young. We also wanted to begin building a power structure for young people in the metro Atlanta area.

We were successful in registering ten thousand young people but not even close to successful in getting those people out to vote. Didn't they understand the importance of voting? Didn't they understand that we had spent a lot of resources, both financial and human, to get them to turn out and have a voice in the election? What was happening? Were young people totally disconnected from our history and the struggle to get the right to vote? Conventional wisdom would argue that they didn't vote because they were young—statistics show that young people don't vote at the levels at which older people vote. I think their age had very little to do with it. I believe young people didn't vote in that election for much the same reasons that many older folks don't vote in current elections. They needed a reason. (I'll get back to my story shortly.)

Having a reason to vote was never an issue for me. I know the importance of voting, first and foremost, because I know my history. I understand the sacrifices that were made for me by people whose names I will never know and who didn't know mine. I understand the importance of voting, because I know that people literally died for me—for us—to have the right to vote. I know the torture, the torment, and the utter disrespect that African Americans, women, and others suffered so that I could get up on Tuesday morning and exercise one of the most important rights afforded to me as a citizen of this country. I know of the blood, sweat, and tears shed so that we could participate as full citizens in our democracy. I think *not* voting is a slap in the face to all of those who thought it important enough to risk everything they had for the right to vote.

If that is not enough (and for some it is not), voting is the one way we can decide who sets policy and what happens when it is passed. It is the difference between whether a child is treated as an adult for certain crimes, or if the color of his skin and the size of his parents' bank account determine that he gets a few months of counseling and no criminal record. Voting determines who picks up your trash and who makes the appointments to United States Supreme Court.

With that stated, I must confess, I find it difficult to understand someone who refuses to vote. Dr. Lowery often says there is a special place in hell for people who don't vote. I agree. (Unless it's a religious thing, and even that I don't understand.) I think a prerequisite to dating should be whether or not a person votes. Why would you want to date someone who is clueless about the world around him or her and how decisions get made? At some point, we have to decide that instead of sitting around complaining about the system, we have to get in and each do our part. For some that means voting and staying engaged after the election; for others it means running for office and, as Ghandi says, becoming "the change you wish to see in the world."

For those who do vote, congratulations. But we often forget the second part to voting—staying engaged in that process and holding elected officials accountable. It means paying attention to the issues you care about and weighing in on them at the appropriate time. If you don't, it widens the disconnect between elected officials and the people they were elected to represent. I don't think elected officials set out to become complacent and disconnected from the communities they represent. I believe that most of us come in wanting to help people and find public policy solutions that can make people's lives better. The problem begins when we are elected and the people who voted for us don't stay engaged and weigh in on the issues important to them.

I don't know if it ever happened in school—we forget the things that we are taught—but it's clear to me that America needs a lesson in Civics 101. It's not just young folks, but people of all ages. There's a general lack of engagement in our country, regardless of age. We need to play a role in the process that determines our quality of life; we can't keep blaming the "politicians" as the reason we don't participate in the process.

Our democracy was created so that we, the people—of all ages, parties, colors, and ideologies—would participate. It was created so that each of us has a voice equal to one another. I think the founders of this country intended for the people to have the power, not the lobbyists or groups with special interests. Whether it's the National Rifle Association or the Teacher's Union, it shouldn't be about the groups and how much money they can offer to political candidates. It should be about the voices of people who vote and pay attention to the process that shapes public policy. We each have a responsibility to be engaged, to help shape our world and environment—not to put elected officials on pedestals, but to hold one another accountable and make this process work for all of us. There is also a responsibility on the part of elected officials to make sure that the people who elected them are informed.

You may ask, "What does this have to do with deciding to run for office?" It has everything to do with running for office. We have enough seat-warming, steak-and–chicken-dinner-eating, deal-making, missing-in-action, elected officials on all levels of government. That reality shouldn't cause you to run away from the political process; it should cause you to run toward it and find your place in it. We need candidates and elected officials who want to be held accountable. We need those who are willing to share their progress and their challenges, to enlist the expertise of the people they represent, and to find ways to open government rather than close it to all except those who are able to write big checks or volunteer on campaigns.

We don't need one more "politician" at any level of our government. I think the deadlock in legislatures and in Congress would strongly suggest we already have too many of those. What we need are more public servants. Public servants look for opportunities to get into a system that has for so long locked out the people it needs most; they must find a way to open the door for everybody. A public servant isn't focused on political games and one-upsmanship, but, rather, on committing him- or herself to transforming how we do business in the body politic. I used to be one of those people who thought I should stay on the outside and raise hell and force change that way. The further I got into the process, the more I realized that, in order to change it, we need people like me and like you on the inside.

Some will ask, why run if the system is broken and too many people are left out? It is broken, but we have to be the ones to fix it. There is a great Buddhist quote that says, "We must know the rules to break them." As servant leaders, community activists, and people who want to do things differently, our job is not to defend the system; it's to make it better. I believe that we have a responsibility to help people see the possibilities, to help them see how things can be rather than how they are now.

I think people who never set out to be elected officials make the best kind of candidates. It takes candidates and elected officials who are willing to make the hard choices, to stand on principles and not change with the wind because they think that position will win the next election. There has to be a sense of responsibility that will renew people's faith—in the system, in our democracy, in people who call themselves elected officials and the electorate—in order to make the process work for themselves. Being responsible even means taking the flack for holding an unpopular position. It means having the courage to do things differently and to be the servant people want to see in their political process. It's a huge burden to carry, but it's what we ask for when we take our oath of responsibility to serve.

When I ran in 2002, I would have been considered an outsider—someone who didn't have all of the proper contacts, didn't know the lingo used within the process, and didn't even know how a bill *really* became a law within the legislative process. I didn't understand the games, the role of lobbyists, the importance of financial support; and I didn't understand why the number of African Americans in a Democratic district mattered so much (I'll explain that in a later chapter). I didn't know all of the ins and outs that insiders know.

That's what helped make me a great candidate. I think it's what makes many people great candidates. I was an outsider who needed to come inside and create change on the inside. Sometimes outsiders have to come inside to make the changes within. It's that quote that you have to know the rules to break them. You have to be inside to learn the rules. Public servants have to be committed to turning the inside out and creating a space that is welcoming for "outsiders."

A servant leader is willing to challenge the status quo because he or she understands that this process has to be shaken up some to allow those who have been marginalized for so long to get a seat at the table. A servant leader is willing to speak truth to power, even if that cuts off his or her financial support from a particular interest. A servant leader is willing to challenge his or her own party when their deeds and their talking points are in direct conflict. And a servant leader remains connected and focused on the people and not necessarily the powerful.

The day of the election in 2001, I got a call from the late Rev. James Orange. Rev. Orange was a legendary civil rights activist who had gone to jail many a day for justice. He spent his career organizing for labor unions around the country. He kept the civil rights community in Georgia connected with the labor movement. He was also the chair of a Voter Empowerment campaign with the People's Agenda (Dr. Lowery's organization). He wanted to know why fewer than thirty people had voted at one of the precincts I was covering. At the time, I couldn't explain why, after all of the work that had been done to register people, so few people had turned out around the city. It wasn't just those that we registered, but people in general who did not take the time to help decide who their government leaders would be. I didn't understand. We were so frustrated. We'd spent all of this energy registering people, talking about the election, and trying to motivate people to go and vote. I didn't get why there was no follow through, why there seemed to be no sense of priority or responsibility. I did discover the reason not long after that day.

I was participating on a panel at Morehouse College. We were talking about the past election and what young people needed to do. At the same time, I had been attending the local community organization meetings in the area where I had moved after graduation. The disconnect became obvious to me. I would sit in these meetings week after week, hearing the same complaints with very little resolution. Many times, we go to community meetings or organize ourselves because there is a problem—sometimes a crisis—that can often be addressed through public policy. We have a problem that we want addressed, but we have no relationship with the elected officials in the community and no real plan on how to get things done to fix our problem. We spin our wheels, talk about how dirty politics is, and stay frustrated until the next problem comes around to focus on.

All of these pieces then came together for me—the work I was doing at the state capitol, my training in the NAACP, my voter empowerment work, my frustration with stagnation in this community group. I also thought it was important for young people to have more of a voice in the legislative process. When visiting the capitol, it seemed as if being close to retirement age or having personal wealth were the two prerequisites for serving. Certainly there were others who did not fit that description, but certainly this seemed to be the majority. It's not that these individuals couldn't represent their constituents, but I knew we needed more of a representation of what the state really looked like. This wasn't just about racial diversity. This was about gender, socio-economic, and ideological diversity. It was about having parents with young children, small business owners, and defense attorneys. It was about a real citizen legislature where the people who serve have the same life experiences as the people they represent.

I knew that there was a void to fill. I knew that voter registration could only go so far, unless people understood that their vote had to go beyond family tradition or even history. Instead, voting had to be about our future; it had to be about the *now*. There was a disconnect for the people in my community group, as there was for people in the municipal election who sat out on Election Day. People weren't making the connection. They didn't understand their power.

I didn't have all of the tools to run for office, the big contacts, or enough training to run a campaign. I had never worked on a campaign, my parents were not politically active other than voting, and no one else in my family had served in political office. I did know that I was tired of going to those same community meetings, hearing those same issues with no resolution. I did know that I had some community support and that I didn't mind working hard. I did have the energy, the new ideas, and the audacity to run in Cobb County of all places. All of those things eventually fell into place (but not without a legal challenge in the midst of it all—I'll share that story later). The most important factors were my heart, my passion, and my experiences working in the community; these could help me help the people I wanted to represent. I was willing to offer myself as a candidate, despite not meeting the "prerequisites" set by conventional wisdom. I also had the ability not to think about the impossibilities. It's one of the things I love about being young.

This is a call for servant leaders—those who have been standing on the sidelines wanting to jump in but feeling afraid that they don't know the big donors or have the strong political connections. This is a call for the community organizer, the PTA president, and the young person who has been registering people to vote—those who have seen the connections between getting involved in the political process, public policy, and their daily lives.

It's hard for working people who simply want to provide for their families and live as productive citizens to understand why they should get involved; some wonder why they should even vote. Having elected officials who only care about re-election further distances those people from their political process and their government. We need community-minded folks who aren't in it for the paycheck, the contract, or the social network-building. We need those who are in it because it's time for those silent voices to be heard; I know that, without you, many of those who control the dialogue don't want those voices to be heard.

What are you waiting for? When you are called to run for office, it's tempting to think that you should wait. When people asked me why I ran so young, I tell them it's because I couldn't wait. I wasn't going to wait my turn, to wait for the district to be more minority or for someone to tap me on the shoulder and tell me it was my turn; and I wasn't going to wait until I had the degrees on the wall, the husband, 2.5 children, and a dog. Those issues that my community faced needed to be dealt with now, and I wasn't going to sit around hoping that someone else would do it. My additional degrees, anointing, or appointing weren't going to create solutions any faster.

I wish I could say that I had known everything about running for office—particularly in Cobb County. Cobb County has a long, checkered history in Georgia. Not only had we never seen an African American serve at the state level, but this was the county that was represented in Congress by Newt Gingrich and Bob Barr. This was the county where the last recorded lynching had taken place—the lynching of a Jewish man, Leo Frank. Cobb County is the place where, in 1996, the Olympics refused to hold events, because the city of Marietta had passed an anti-gay resolution. At that time, it seemed Cobb County was the home of conservatism and exclusion. Among black people outside the county, it was known as "Cop" County or "Snob" County. Even today, it has a reputation for police who stop black men when they enter the county.

With all that history, you can imagine why my announcement to run was comical for some. Honestly, at the time, I didn't know all of that history. Neither did I know that those would be reasons that any reasonable person wouldn't even consider running. I learned that not knowing turned out to be a pretty good thing. When you don't know there are limits, you are less likely to be defined or confined by them. That's what happened with my decision to run in Cobb County. I never actually thought about whether an African American had ever been elected to the legislature or any other law-making body. I simply knew that this was a way I could help resolve some of the issues faced by people in my community. I knew that there was obviously a need for someone from our community to be elected so that people could feel connected with their government and, hence, public policy decisions.

There was a lot that I didn't know about the process of running or even what the response would be. Once I started telling people, though, I quickly found out. I started going to different community events and announcing that I was going to run for office. The reception was different in each place. I remember telling one of my now-colleagues from Atlanta, who smiled and was so amused that she thought it important to tell the rest of the people at an event I was attending. It was almost as if she wanted to be the first to share the joke that this little black girl was running in Cobb County—and against an incumbent, at that.

Initially, I was going to have to run against the incumbent in my district. I was fine with that, considering that, when I looked at his last two elections, fewer than seven hundred people had voted. In fact, I believe it was around five hundred. I didn't know all of the details of to how to win an election, but I figured I could certainly get more than five hundred votes. A lot more people in the district are voting now. In my last primary election almost three thousand votes were cast in my race.

I remember announcing my intentions at a state NAACP event, and the crowd was excited. There were offers of checks right there on the spot. When I started telling people in Cobb, there was a mixed response. Some were very excited, and others didn't quite know what it meant. The most fun was attending my first Cobb Democratic Party meeting. Of the two hundred people in the room, about ten were black. It was clear that they weren't used to seeing black candidates.

There was also a group of people, both in Cobb County and out, who smiled and thought it was very cute that I was running. They all but patted me on the head and said, "You're going to have a nice experience." They simply didn't think it was possible. Of course, I had a small group of people who were so bold as to tell me that it wasn't possible. I had a couple of the old folks who gave the "you haven't paid your dues" speech. They said that Cobb County wouldn't elect a black woman, and certainly not a young black woman. Some even joked that there weren't enough black people to even vote for me. That might have been partially true, but I was trying to represent the whole district, not just black people.

With that kind of stained history (which does not tell the whole story of who and what Cobb County is), you can understand why people thought it would be nothing but an "experience" for me to run. They just couldn't fathom how a county with that kind of reputation would elect a young black woman who wasn't even from there.

I continued to do my research to figure out how this could be done. I started going to all kinds of candidate and campaign trainings. I didn't have any campaign staff or volunteers yet, but I wanted to develop an understanding of the task ahead. I knew that the race issue was a real one. I also knew that it would take skill to understand how to run a campaign, and, despite what the odds were, I needed to have the knowledge to be successful. Running for office is a science. As qualified as I believed I was, I needed to learn how to win. As time went on, not only did I get a real understanding of what it takes to be successful when running for office, but I also learned how ugly it could get.

After filing all of the necessary papers, I started getting my team together. Most of them lived outside of Cobb County, and none of us had ever run a political campaign before. Tharon Johnson, with whom I had just finished working on the big voter registration project, was now a close friend. He took the first few steps with me, helping me navigate the mechanics of a campaign, helped me put a team together, and was one of the people I needed around me who was crazy enough to think it was a good idea for me to run for office. We started meeting at my house. We had a campaign kickoff, and all of five people were there. That didn't discourage us.

About a month or so into the campaign, I had to get a campaign manager. Tharon was only temporary, and it wasn't working, because we continued to have personality conflicts and power struggles. That was my first lesson about choosing appropriate staff and people I could work with and in what capacity. I learned that not all of your friends should manage your affairs and campaigns or be involved in your business affairs. Those dynamics are crucial and have to be considered before you make such important decisions.

This doesn't mean that Tharon wasn't a phenomenal friend. In fact, he was. When I had to take time off from work to campaign, it was Tharon who paid my bills for a month and made sure I had what I needed to stay focused on the campaign. Everybody has a role, and, without Tharon, I would've had to find a way to keep the lights on that month. Tharon and I are still great friends, and he remains one of the most important people in my inner circle. Since then, he has gone on to manage and help elect one of the best mayors I believe Atlanta will ever see, Kasim Reed.

We found another manager/campaign consultant who lived in Cobb County. He fit the mold I thought was necessary to go into circles I wouldn't have direct access to. I thought he would be the person to carry me to victory—that was, until I found out one day that he was no longer my campaign manager. The fact is, he had put someone else in the race with the same last name and filed a residency challenge against me. That was my first lesson in how ugly things could get. I still don't understand how that all took place. I do understand why. That experience would be the one to help define my story.

Tharon found someone who was willing to take on my campaign. He was a twenty-one-year-old college student who had worked on one other campaign. Rashad Taylor is his name. We knew each other from campus work with NAACP. He was a Morehouse student while I was at Spelman. We had only interacted a few times, but Tharon assured me that this guy was going to take me to victory. I believed him and accepted Rashad as my manager. On his first day on the campaign, he rearranged all the furniture and turned my house into a campaign headquarters. That was my first clue that he was serious and might even have known what he was doing.

While working with Rashad and the consultants who developed our campaign plan for him to implement, we had this ugly court case questioning my residency hovering over our heads. Before people started finding out about that, I'd been more successful at raising the necessary funds to run the campaign. I had support from some of the women's groups and a few courageous supporters like—none other than—Dr. Lowery, who didn't pat me on the head and tell me about the good experience I would gain. He contributed one thousand dollars to my campaign and told me I could do it. There were a few others along the way who were willing to invest in me and my campaign early on.

Once the media caught wind of my candidacy, I began getting a lot of press. The newspapers, and even local television stations, covered my campaign and a few other young people who were also running for the legislature. The local newspaper in my county also started running stories about my residency challenge.. I thought those stories would be the end of my campaign. I thought people would read them and not even consider my candidacy, much less vote for me.

Despite the articles in the local and Atlanta papers, we continued to run the campaign and try to raise money; and Rashad continued to make me knock on doors daily. That was the routine, and we were not going to veer from it. There were times when I felt discouraged and could finally understand why people were skeptical about my chances.

In the eyes of others, I was in over my head. I remember one of the old folks, one who was never supportive, telling me that there was no way I could beat this residency issue and that I needed to give up. She had always been discouraging me, telling me and others that I had not paid my dues and had no right to run for office. In fact, the night before we went to court, she left a message on my voicemail telling me that I would lose and needed to get out of the race. Those were her words.

The residency issue at hand was created because of the redrawing of the lines in the legislature. This is also called the redistricting or reapportionment process. This takes place every ten years after the census is complete to consider growth in population. The Georgia legislature had redrawn the lines at the same time that I lived in an apartment in Cobb County about five minutes away from the house that I would buy when I was twenty-one years old. I had known that I was going to run, so, when I bought the house, I bought it in the same area and same legislative district. After putting a contract on the house, the closing date was moved back several times. When the United States Justice Department approved newly-drawn lines to create additional seats in the district, my old apartment and the new house were no longer in the same district. An argument could be made that I had not lived long enough in the "new" district I was running in.

One month before the primary election, I stood before the judge who had to decide whether I had lived in the district for the one year required. In my mind, with new maps, no one had lived in the district long enough, because they were new districts. I also knew that I had moved only five minutes away, and both places were in the same legislative district. That was the first time I realized how much support I had from people all around the Atlanta area. The courtroom was filled with friends. Rev. James Orange was there. State Representative and longtime activist Tyrone Brooks was there, along with many others.

They stood with me through that entire experience. I will never forget that.

We put together character witnesses (as if that had anything to do with residency) and had all of the paperwork we thought would help. I hired the lawyer with the best reputation in election law, and he presented my case. I remember almost everything about that day. My mom even flew in from Miami to be there for me. I can remember the suit I was wearing, which was one of my yellow campaign suits. I wanted to brighten the room and leave a positive impression with the judge. After we presented the case, the judge let us know that we would get the decision soon. We didn't know the exact time frame, but were hoping we would know in a matter of days so that we could have enough time before the election to determine our course of action.

Much to all of our disappointment, days went by and we had no decision. Two and a half weeks went by and there was still no decision. I continued to knock on doors and attempted to raise money, all while having to pay a lawyer. It was now twelve days before the election. Finally, I was driving down I-20 again, and I got a call from the newspaper. They wanted to know how I felt now that I was no longer in the race. We had lost the residency challenge.

I was absolutely shocked. I had never been in a situation remotely like this. I had people who had contributed to the campaign, volunteers who were working every single day to help me get elected. How was I going to go home and face these people? What was I going to say? The tears rolled down my face. I immediately got on the phone and called my boyfriend at the time, who is now my husband. I started questioning God. I wondered what I had done to deserve this. It seemed like, as soon as I found out, everyone else did, too. I started getting calls from everyone imaginable. Overwhelmingly, people were saying I should drop this and move on with my life. They told me that fighting this would just ruin my "career." Even my campaign manager, who now regrets it, told me that I should just wait and run in two years. I didn't know what I was going to do at that very moment, but it was all too much to fathom at one time.

David and I went to Red Lobster. Red Lobster is my favorite restaurant in the entire world. I have been going there on my own since I was sixteen years old, weekly. Yes, with the exception of traveling to South Africa for two weeks in 2004, I go to Red Lobster at least once a week, sometime two to three times a week. I go to Red Lobster to celebrate as well as when I need cheering up. This occasion screamed for a Red Lobster virgin sunset passion drink, and I needed to be there.

The calls continued to come in while I tried to decide what to do next. We had the option of appealing this decision or accepting the ruling of the judge and being out of the race. Whatever the decision was, the Cobb Board of Elections was now placing signs outside their offices that "Alisha Thomas" had been removed from the ballot. We had to make a decision fast with all of the factors considered. I listened to call after call, and I even made some calls to some of my biggest supporters, wanting their opinions. I weighed the options of staying in or dropping out. Even my consultants told me that I shouldn't worry about it; I could run again in two years. I remember calling my mother, and her biggest concern was not having another loss. She couldn't deal with seeing me go through this hurt again if we decided to appeal the case. She was with me either way. Like any good mother, she just didn't want to see her baby hurt. I appreciated all of the support from my friends and family.

That day, I learned what the decision would have to be about. It would have to be about the people I wanted to represent. I knew the decision had to be about what would happen if I moved out of the way and allowed the very people who had created this challenge to represent my community. I thought about all of the issues that needed to be addressed and all of the people who remained locked out and disconnected from the process. I considered all of the people who had told me to wait; and, at that moment, I realized that waiting was not an option.

Dr. Martin Luther King Jr. wrote what I believe is the most powerful commentary on what happens when we wait in his letter from the Birmingham jail. He talks about preachers and members of faith community who wanted him to wait a little while longer before he took on the Jim Crow laws. He raises the critical point for all of us about waiting for the "right" time. In my case, people were advising me that for the sake of my "career," I needed to wait. What they didn't realize was that my running had nothing to do with a political career. It was not about planning this life in politics that would elevate me to the next position. My decision to run was about adding a voice in the legislature that was willing to challenge the status quo. It was about addressing head-on the real issues that people faced; and, for many, waiting was not an option.

I asked myself how long people should wait before they get the kind of education every child deserves. How long should people wait before they have elected officials who are willing to roll up their sleeves and get the job done? How long? I remember what it felt like when the tears rolled down my face, and how powerless I felt. I knew that my running wasn't about me, but about the people who believed in the impossible. I knew that running was about change and challenging the status quo. It was then that I realized what happens when you wait for the right time, the right situation, the right number of children, degrees on the wall. You never get around to it, because there is rarely a time when all of the ingredients for the "right time" will be there at the same time.

Instead, when you are called to do something, whatever it is, the time is now. We can't wait for someone else to do it.

We decided I would appeal the case. I called my lawyer and gave him the news. I remember him giving me the full disclosure answer that we "didn't necessarily have the legal arguments to fight this." In fact, he didn't know how we were going to win this, but he was going to search for more legal precedents. He was going to do everything he could. That was fine, and I appreciated his service. I knew, though, that the one who would make the final decision would do all He could. This was a Friday, and the lawyer would have to file the case immediately to get in court on that Monday. He did.

We went before the second judge, and my memory of all of the details are less descriptive. I remember that waiting to get into the courtroom was like waiting for what seemed like days and weeks. The group with us was much smaller. In the back of my mind, I kept thinking that we were a week away from the election, people were voting on absentee ballots, and my name would not appear on the ballots. I was in a three-way race with two other men who were white and twice my age. I believed I needed every vote I could get and this situation was ruining my chances.

We presented the case, and, rather than making us wait weeks or even hours, that judge overturned the decision right then and there. He ruled, not on the merits of the case, but on the fact that the challenge was done by fax and therefore not filed properly. Some would call that a lucky technicality. I call that God's divine order. I call that beating the odds. When something is meant to happen in the universe, there are forces that may slow it down but cannot completely stop it.

The next day, I was back on the front of the newspaper; but this time the headlines had changed. This time the story had to say that I was back in the race. It was an unbelievable experience. I didn't have too much time to focus on it, because we were one week away from the election; it was time to take off that suit and get back in the community to earn some votes.

I went straight to the Cobb Board of Elections and got the list of people who had already turned in absentee ballots. I was able to call them and let them know that they could recast their vote in my race, now that I was no longer disqualified. The response was lukewarm at best. No one seemed interested in making any changes to their ballot. Truth be told, these were older white people who were voting absentee, and, quite frankly, that was not my base. I stopped that process and focused on the folks who had not yet cast their ballots. We might have gone to Red Lobster that night to celebrate. I don't actually remember. Our campaign had learned a lesson in faith, perseverance, and seeing the impossible happen; and we would never be the same.

One week later on August 20, 2002, we woke up at 6:00 am. It was Election Day. We had the residency issue behind us, and we had carried out every piece of the plan. We had volunteers at my house, ready to work all day to make history in Cobb County. We could feel victory in the air. We didn't believe that's what it was, because we had been told for so long that what we were trying to do was impossible. I remember standing on the busy intersections, waving with my signs, and people would honk and yell, "I voted for you." I thought, *There are too many people saying that; they must not be saying that just to make me feel good.*

We continued to campaign until the polls closed at 7:00. The core campaign team drove over to the official county watch site and waited for the results to come in. The local newspaper reporter and photographer were there to capture the story and picture of whatever the outcome was. It seemed like forever, waiting for the numbers to come in. After ten o'clock that night, we had finally gotten enough of the numbers to know what the outcome was going to be.

In a three-way race where I was the only young person, only woman, and only African American; in the race in Cobb County where so many people had said it was impossible, that the odds were stacked against me because my skin was too dark, my age too young, and my thoughts too liberal; in the county that had lynched Leo Frank and given us Newt Gingrich and Bob Barr, I won the election with almost 65 percent of the vote.

Our faces were beaming with pride and joy and even a little disbelief. That little team of five people, all under thirty years old, had beaten the odds in Cobb County. I went on to win the general election that November against Andy Bush—no relation to George W. Bush. I got over 55 percent in what was considered a swing district that wasn't meant for me. We had accomplished the impossible.

Not only had we taught ourselves a lesson in faith and seeing the impossible become possible, but we had also shown other people what can happen when you just believe. I also learned that Cobb County was more than just part of a dark history. It was a growing, more inclusive county, where people were willing to vote for a young woman from Miami, Florida, putting aside race and even age. It's a county I am proud to represent and proud to call home.

My first election was one of the most important experiences in my life. It taught me the importance of having faith in myself and faith in God. That experience taught me a lot of lessons about listening to my core and walking in my purpose. It taught me the importance of taking in wise counsel but never letting go of what my gut and heart say to do. Those people who were advising me to let go and try again next time didn't mean me any harm. They were simply trying to protect my heart from any more pain and disappointment. They were simply trying to help me look at the reality and the odds of the situation. I respect them for that. I learned that what God has for you is for you. It doesn't matter what the odds are, what other people say is possible or impossible.

I also learned that we simply cannot wait when we have been called to do something. I can't help but think about my favorite quote in this instance by Dr. Benjamin E. Mays: "Every person is born into this world to do something distinctive and something unique, and, if he or she does not do it, it will never be done." Imagine all of the people who were born to make the world we live in a better place. Imagine all of the skeptics and realists who surrounded them, who told them it was impossible. Imagine the many stumbling blocks, many of them legal, others physical—like dogs, water hoses, and police officers. Think about where we would be if these people had never been born. Imagine what life would be like if they had waited for the right time or for someone else to do it. Imagine if they had believed that their assignment was too hard and had surely been given to the wrong person. Imagine if they had realized what all of the limitations were.

We all have to think about what blocks we allow to be put in our way—blocks that keep us from moving in our purpose. For some people, their purpose is starting a business or a career in teaching. For others it is going back to school. For some it is following the path that they are passionate about, but they are afraid of what people will say or what it will do to their social status. Some people are afraid they don't have all of the tools and information to make their purpose happen.

Whatever is blocking you, you must take in this lesson of making the impossible possible. You have to go within your core, gut, and heart and reconnect with your purpose. You can't wait for all of the pieces to be perfectly aligned. Instead, you have to step out in faith and realize that, though there will be stumbling blocks and people who will laugh or think it will be a "nice learning experience" for you, it is what you have been told to do. If you don't do it, it will never be done.

For those of us who have been called into service, we sometimes wish we had hung up the phone. It's easier to close your heart and reside in the world where ignorance is bliss. The only problem is, as Dr. Mays reminds us, "If we don't do it, it will never be done." There are days that I get tired and want to go home, lock the doors, and never come out. There are days when I want to turn off my phone (there are rare occasions when I do) and not accept calls for a while.

For those of us who still have a lot of work to do, we have to dust off our bottoms and get up and fight for another day. We have to find ways to encourage ourselves and one another. We have to take some time to go back to why we decided to do this work in the first place. We have to rekindle the fire we have in our hearts, to get back on the battlefield and keep fighting. We all get discouraged, and there will be times when it seems like the end is nowhere in sight. We have to remember that this is not a hundred-yard dash; this is a marathon. The race doesn't end as soon as we would like it to, but, at the end of the race, we know it was worth all of the long nights and all of the preparation up to that point.

On those days when I get tired and too overwhelmed to go on, I stop. I take a "me" day or half-day. I may take a bubble bath or go to a movie by myself, just to relieve my mind of all of the burdens I'm carrying. Whatever you do to relax and refocus, do it. We have to take time for ourselves to renew our minds and spirits. The phones and Blackberries continue to ring, and the e-mails continue to come. If we don't take care of ourselves, we cannot take care of the people we are called to serve. Do what it takes for you to get back in shape to get up another day. Those moments when you are on the brink of giving up, think about the people who inspire you. Think about the struggles of the civil rights or women's rights movements, when the circumstances were even more difficult than what we face. If they could get through it, then so can we.

It is a heavy burden to carry the troubles of others on your shoulders. It is also an incredible feeling to know that you are in a position to change the circumstances of individuals and entire groups of people. Recall the fulfillment you have felt when you saw the smile on faces of those you have been able to help. Those are the experiences we should draw upon to continue in this journey. You and I have been called, and I am glad that we have answered.

❀ LESSONS I LEARNED ALONG THE WAY ❀

1. **Never apologize or ask permission to run for office or move to the next level.** Real leaders don't wait for someone to anoint them to move forward with their vision, especially when they know they are qualified to do the job. Sometimes we are the person who presents the biggest obstacle, because we are waiting for someone to bless the job we have been called to do.

2. **"Make your haters your motivators."** A former Atlanta radio personality used to say this all the time. We can't spend our time focusing on or removing from our lives the people who mean us harm. Whether the haters are old people or our peers, choose not to focus on their negativity and lack of vision. Remember, they can't see what you can see. Instead, turn that hate into motivation. Let their words of discouragement become the fire you need to work harder, to run faster and get better at what you do.

3. **Challenge the status quo.** The longer we are in a situation, the more comfortable we can become. Sometimes we keep doing things that don't seem to work, because we don't know there is another way. Conventional wisdom should be respected, but it should also be built upon by those who are unconventional. That's you. Never accept what others say is possible. Create your own possibilities.

4. **Don't allow stumbling blocks to keep you away from your purpose.** Creating change is never easy. People will place obstacles in your way, and sometimes they are beyond anyone's control. Those

obstacles are not there to overcome you. Most times those obstacles are there to prepare you for the real battles ahead. If you aren't strong enough to handle the little battles, how will you be prepared for the war?

5. Know the rules so you know how to break them. Learn the game, not to become a player, but to learn how to undo the rules and challenge the status quo. Knowing the rules and even understanding how or why decisions are made helps us to create the change we want to see from the inside out.

6. Stop waiting. Quit waiting for the right time, the right circumstance, and the perfect combination to move forward. Life doesn't usually allow us to have all of the money, power, time, degrees, children, or personal desires all at once before we move into leadership or take the step we need to take in life. Whether it's running for office, going back to school, creating a nonprofit, or starting a business, stop allowing excuses or an imperfect set of circumstances to keep you away from your destiny.

7. Participate in the process. Whether you decide to run for office, become a citizen lobbyist, or become a poll worker, our country was built on a democracy in which everyone can participate in some way. Public policy is a powerful tool that can change our quality of life. Don't allow the people who are willing to participate decide the quality of life you get because you allow them to make all of the decisions and choose not to make your voice heard.

8. Trust that when you are called to do something you will have everything you need. After you decide that waiting is not an excuse, have faith that God will provide you with everything you need. That does not come without work and seeking those tools. We all know the Bible scripture (even if you aren't a Christian) that says *faith without works is dead*. This doesn't mean to make the decision and wait while everything falls from the sky; it means, if you are walking in your destiny and are working toward your calling (working is the operative word), everything you need to be successful will be available to you. It's up to you to utilize those resources.

6. SNATCHING THE TORCH: BRIDGING THE GAP

WHETHER IT WAS MY FIRST run for office or my experiences today in the legislature, the most vocal opposition and biggest challenges come from older people. I'm not suggesting that all old people have problems with young people. That has not been my experience. What has been my experience is the constant struggle with those old folks who just can't get over their own issues with younger people who have new ideas and a different way of looking at things. How often have young leaders been in a room with older people, offered an idea that gets shot down, only to have the same idea raised by an older person—and, all of a sudden, it's the best thing since sliced bread? It happens way too often.

The first time I discovered the hypocrisy of some of our civil rights leaders was during a civil rights trip in Birmingham, Alabama. I had traveled with a large group to walk the path of the Bloody Sunday March from Selma to Montgomery. I was about twenty-one at the time and had recently graduated from Spelman. The march over the bridge was a highlight of the trip for me after learning about John Lewis and Hosea Williams and many other young people during that time who braved dogs, water hoses, and billy clubs, seeking the right to vote. We watched videos, visited road markers where several incidents had occurred, and constantly heard about the role young people played during the civil rights movement.

I remember learning about students who sat in at lunch counters in North Carolina; I learned how young people were the fearless ones during the movement, ready to go to jail and endure violent attacks, despite their own nonviolence. I recalled all of these things as we prepared to cross the infamous Edmund Pettis Bridge that weekend. As we lined up, taking to the streets of Selma, a group of young people decided to make our way up to the front of the line. We were filled with excitement and pride as young people because it was *we* who had stood on the front lines. Only when we got to the front of the line to take what we thought was our rightful and symbolic place, we were told to get back. There were some old folks who needed to take to the front lines—not because they were there originally, but because it simply wasn't our place. It was like a slap in the face.

That experience had to have been close to ten years ago, but it still burns deep in my heart. We were embarrassed and deflated. I still remember that moment because it was a reminder that when old folks say that young people are the leaders of tomorrow, they mean it—literally. It's like when I was growing up; my parents told me I would get something tomorrow, but tomorrow never became *today*. For old people who constantly tell young people they are the leaders of tomorrow, that's exactly what they mean.

I have to make the distinction borrowed from one of my big brothers, Jeff Johnson. Jeff was the National Youth Director of the NAACP during the time I was the Spelman College chapter president. He coined the distinction that I often use to define the difference between old folks and elders. My reference to "old folks" refers to those who sit around reminiscing about the "movement" as if it's over. They talk about how things were back then and have yet to do more than talk in the present day. They romanticize the movement and give the impression that everyone was involved in it.

Old folks are intimidated by young people and believe that there is no such thing as passing a torch. If no one who passed one to them, they aren't passing one to us. Old folks don't make the connection that they were my age and even younger when they were challenging the status quo and Jim Crow laws. It has yet to dawn on them that, rather than looking down on young people, they ought to find ways to help us, teach us, and even work with us, instead of *talking* about how things used to be in their day.

I remember speaking to the wife of a well-known civil rights leader. It was my first time meeting her. I was excited and honored to speak with her, only to be berated for not understanding the movement and scolded for all that was wrong with young people today. I wasn't necessarily expecting a pat on the back. I *was* hoping for some encouraging words or some advice on how to be successful in our work. Although I know I need to let that experience go, I still have hard feelings toward her because it was a missed opportunity to bridge the gap that keeps different generations from working together. I know I'm not the only young person starry-eyed over some civil rights icon, only to be shot down with a lecture about all that's wrong with my generation.

I participated in a panel discussion a few years back with about ten other young people from around the country who were all standing on the front lines in our own ways. In came a well-known civil rights leader who listened in on the conversation for a while. When asked if he was ready to pass the torch, he pointed out that there was no torch and, if there was, he had worked hard to get his. He said nobody had passed anything to him, and he wasn't getting out of the way for anybody. I am paraphrasing, but the message was very clear. We were all struck by his comments and, of course, disappointed. Obviously, he had created a space for young people to have a voice by having the panel. That was great, but how much more beneficial could it have been if we were interfacing with the generation before us to talk about what real leadership is?

As a young person on the front lines in the Georgia legislature, these experiences burn like a hot iron to the soul. It's discouraging and deflating. It's not that young people are looking for a parade, or even applause, for the work we do. We are looking for that second category of people that Jeff calls elders, those who are willing to teach young people and learn from them at the same time. Elders are those like my hero, Dr. Joseph Lowery, who is not intimidated by young people. Instead, they spend time giving advice, sharing their stories, and helping young people along the way to understand their role and the significance of all people in the movement. Elders are not afraid to talk about the movement of the past and the present, about how critical it is to get rid of turf battles and obsession with nostalgia, the old days, and how things "used" to be.

Elders understand that the struggle is not yet over and there is enough work for all of us to do. They don't give long speeches about how you haven't paid your dues to run for office or hold a position. Instead, they take you under their wings and teach you the ropes. They aren't intimidated to stand side-by-side with you or share a podium with you at a program. The true elders seek opportunities for your continued growth, and they don't sit around hoping that you fail because you didn't kiss their ring or ask their permission to move.

What would have happened to the young people who were told to move to the back at the march in Alabama if they had allowed that affront to discourage them? What would have happened to that young woman who was insulted and berated by the wife of the civil rights leader if she had internalized those words and allowed that experience to dishearten her? What would have happened to those young leaders in the room if they had believed the people—even some they looked up to—who said they weren't good enough, weren't prepared, and weren't old enough to do the work they were doing? Old people have to come out of their nostalgia and welcome the folks who are willing to take the risks that they themselves are simply too old (in their own minds) and too tired to take.

In fairness, I think it's important to acknowledge that there are young people who have no regard for history or the contributions that our elders have made, and who have no interest in learning it. I am embarrassed by them, because they, too, contribute to the generation gap. It's they who give other young people a bad name and keep perpetuating the stereotypes that we are disconnected from our history, are apathetic, and lack commitment to our communities. They are the socially unconscious brothers who rap about trap houses and whores and women whose goals are to be a video queen or an athlete's wife. It's the small sector of our generation whose focus is on bling, getting paid, or just getting laid.

The result is a gap where generations aren't passing information; they are passing blame. It's unfortunate and real. The old folks talk about the young folks, and young people too often talk about how old people just don't understand, that they are out of touch and just want things to go back to the way they used to be rather than looking forward. Old people end up feeling hopeless, and young people end up figuring out things for themselves.

The more I talk to young professionals, the more I realize that this generation gap exists in different sectors. Too often, I hear stories about young professionals under forty who have "made it" but with very little help from their older counterparts. The stories are painfully similar across the country, stories of young people feeling frustrated about not getting the kind of help and support that they need to get ahead. Instead, they are told to wait their turn, earn it, or pay their dues. They say, "I want you to climb your way up without any help, like I did. I want you to feel the pain so you can appreciate it like I do." It's like they take pride in watching those who come after them struggle to get ahead.

We also need to deal with the gender issue within the generational divide. Throughout my travels and conversations with young people in my generation, I find that gender plays a role in how we advance professionally, and even politically. When I first ran for office, it was mostly men who embraced my candidacy, wrote the first checks, and took the time to take me around to meet people and teach me the ropes. It was mostly the women who said I wasn't ready, that I hadn't paid my dues—and questioned why I even thought I could or should run. Ironically, the woman who was most hostile toward me—the one who left that message on my voicemail the night before the court case—is the founder of an organization that supports black women.

It seems that this is pretty commonplace in my generation. I'm not sure if this is just an issue in the black community, but I've met too many young black women who have started their own organizations and networking groups because they felt the older women in their lives were threatened by them—thought they were after their jobs or even their men. These women were less likely to give advice or share any information to help the younger woman get ahead. Some were just plain destructive, trying to ensure that they could hold on to the little power and position they had. Conversely, I heard one very successful young black man who credited black women for his success. I've heard other young black men talk about the women in their lives who have helped them get to where they are. However, I have also seen young black men have a hard time connecting to their older counterparts for the mentorship and support they seek to get ahead. Why is that?

Some would say it's simply a matter of attraction, even sexual attraction. While I won't discount that as a factor for some, I can't say in my situation that every older black man that sought to help me *wanted* me. That certainly was a factor for one or two of them, and may have been a factor for more, but I never compromised myself or my values to get support from any of these men. I think the same argument can be made for the guys who got help from older women.

Sometimes I think it's the dynamic between black mothers and their sons, black men and their daughters. It's the "mama's boy" or "daddy's little girl" syndrome combined with all of the other social factors affecting black men and women in our society. Think about mothers and sons and the relationships between them. Whether single or married, black mothers tend to "raise" their daughters, ensure that they can be independent, fend for themselves, and can thrive in any environment. We are told to maintain our own bank accounts (oops, was I supposed to keep that a secret?) and learn how to change a tire or at least keep all of the tools in our cars. We are taught early how to balance a checkbook, how to hem. We are taught to make sure we learn all we can and become self-sufficient. We are taught to be resourceful and depend on no man or thing to get us to where we want to be in life.

On the other hand, those black women who were fortunate to have an active father present in the home were also taught that Daddy could fix everything. They learned that when they messed up, they could just call Daddy. When something broke down in the house, Daddy could fix it. They taught us to just sit back because Daddy could handle it and get us where we needed to go. Even in my adult age, I still call my daddy when something goes wrong in the house or I need to make a decision about my car. These messages from our parents are often life-long.

I do not attempt to speak for black men. I don't profess to understand all of the many complexities of living in America as a black man. While black women were raised to be independent, black men seem to have been coddled and encouraged to depend on their moms or some beautiful and smart sister to take care of their needs. If this is true, it might explain why older black men are more likely to help young women, and older black women are more likely to help young black men. Black women could very well see young black men as their sons, coddling and helping them along the way, making sure they're successful. Older black men could very well see young black women as their daughters, helping them fix their problems.

Maybe it's just the competition factor. Like the older women who work with my friends, they see younger women as competition and don't want to provide any opportunities for their place to be taken. Rather than share information, these men and women want to hold on to it to mark their territory. I don't think it's by accident that not one woman offered to help me find my way in the legislature when I first got there. Even now, some of them are willing to talk *about* me, but they rarely talk *to* me about how I can get better at what I do. For the record, there are women who have been incredibly supportive of my political efforts, Deane Bonner, president of the Cobb NAACP, and Helen Butler, executive director of Georgia Coalition for the People's Agenda. This lack of support is a stark difference from growing up and being surrounded by black women who invested a great deal of their time and guidance to ensure my success. It is frustrating to me and to others, and it continues to widen the generation gap where young and old people feel a sense of resentment toward one another.

I would be remiss if I did not acknowledge that the black community is not the only group of people who suffer because the old people won't get out of the way. I've seen the same thing happen within the Democratic Party. It seems like Republicans are great at creating the bench and, in my experience, giving young people encouragement and opportunities in leadership. The bench refers to a line of people who are ready when their appointed time comes to take on the position they've been trained to do. The investment of time and knowledge has been put in by elders who want to see a young person succeed. The bench suggests that there is a process in place that is strategic and deliberate, where young people are given the skills, the know-how, and the exposure to take on the positions of those before them.

We don't see this bench in the civil rights community, and I haven't seen it in Democratic politics. Few people over forty talk about, or even acknowledge, the need for a bench on the Democratic side. It's why we are shuffling every two to four years, looking for candidates to run for legislative, statewide seats or even leadership positions within their elected capacities. I sit in caucus meetings as the strategy is being devised, "Find the retired teachers and military personnel." They think retirees are the people with the time, and sometimes the resources, to run for office. They completely ignore young people and don't even consider training a young person who could run at some point in the future. Instead, they only see them as good campaign workers or legislative aides, not strong candidates with energy and insight to help breathe life into what we do.

The people who fail to teach and help prepare the bench are the same ones who won't stop and evaluate why their approach isn't working. They don't listen to anyone whose life experiences don't match theirs and don't realize that their sometimes antiquated approach can't work for new times. For them, it's more within their own conventional wisdom to stick with the strategy that worked for them for the last thirty years. The consequences are that people stay in their coveted positions too long, wearing out their welcome and, in some cases, their relevancy. They literally die in their positions with no one to step up behind them.

The conventional wisdom behind this is that they get to keep their position as long as they want, because they don't want to give up the power, nor do they want to lose their relevance in the process. They feel that if they help someone else, they could lose what they've worked their entire lives for. This perpetuates the disconnect between young and old as well and keeps us employing the same old tired tactics, netting the same old tired results. It hurts the legacy of the community, organization, political agenda, and—worst of all—the movement. It also creates a sense of resentment for people who want to get involved but feel shut out of the process.

We saw this in the presidential election with Barack Obama. Early on, we learned that the 2008 election wasn't just going to be about the war, the economy, and public education. It was also going to force generations within different communities to face the big elephant in the room. It was the generation gap. The "old" folks lined up for the Clintons without question. I say the Clintons because I believe that many of them were tied to the former president and felt a sense of obligation out of loyalty. Ironically, the vast majority of elders lined up to support Barack Obama.

It forced many of us to ask ourselves some important questions. Was it about race for those of us who supported Barack Obama? Was it about loyalty and a sense of owing the Clintons, rather than supporting the kind of candidate they say they worked all of their lives to see? Was it about gender for those women who felt they had to support Hillary Clinton? Was it that Barack Obama hadn't paid his dues?

It even forced us to ask questions about others we considered to be leaders in our community. We found elected officials, those who had been considered cutting edge by some, fall on the "wrong" side of this decision. Longstanding elected officials were challenged for the first time in years and, for some, the first time ever, because they were considered out of touch for supporting Clinton over Obama. Those of us who were on the "right" side from the beginning didn't understand why there was even a choice. We had one candidate who represented change and hope, and another who represented much of the same. Eventually, I believed that even our most courageous leaders chose the wrong side, because sometimes you can become part of an institution for so long that you don't even realize it. It's hard to support a change in status quo when you *are* status quo.

For those leaders in the civil rights community who chose the Clintons over Barack Obama, they found themselves caught in a quandary. We were all baffled about their choice, and, yes, their relevance in the modern-day movement for change. We had to challenge them about their position, because all along we thought we were fighting to challenge the status quo. We thought we were standing together in solidarity to shake up the "plantation," if you will. I'm not suggesting that any person who chose Clinton over Obama sold us out or were necessarily wrong. I am saying that too many old folks were on the wrong side for what I believe were the wrong reasons. That's problematic when the goal is to move forward as a country.

It was a challenging moment in our history. It shed light on this generation gap as we looked at younger people or people with a newer approach who were desperate to see our country move in a different direction. We yearned for a new approach and supported Obama, and many of the old-school people who seemed to simply want more of the same supported Clinton. We all had to look at ourselves and do a check on what we say our values are, what we really want to accomplish, and what path will get us there.

As Frederick Douglass once said, there is no "progress without struggle." We needed to struggle through that moment so that we could examine what real leadership is. It made us all think about what we were fighting for. Were we putting race and gender before content of character, ability, and vision? It was about Obama's ability to bring people together, not divide them. It was about the future of this country, not the old favors or reliving the past or even the money some would get in return for their support for the Clintons. It wasn't supposed to be that Obama didn't get their permission first or go into the proverbial dark room where the decisions get made and come out with their blessing. It made us have to be honest about what was important and put our pride and personal agendas aside.

It seemed like most of the old people who supported Clinton over Obama were more focused on telling him to wait his turn, to pay more dues, to give them just a little more time in the limelight. I wanted to tell those out-of-touch "leaders" that they didn't have to worry about their place in history. They didn't have to worry about losing their place in the spotlight, because no one can ever take away the countless number of selfless acts carried out in the name of justice and equality. They didn't have to think that, because there was a new name and face, they weren't still relevant and necessary.

I wanted to tell those leaders that their work to move this country and, in many cases, the world forward will never be forgotten. We could never take away from their lives of sacrifice and their contributions that had carried us to this moment. Too many people gave up their opportunities in private industry, careers with benefits and pension plans, and lives of luxury—or just life without threats to their lives and livelihoods. We could never adequately repay, or forget, all of the things they gave up so that we could sit wherever we want on buses, live in the neighborhoods of our choice, eat at lunch counters, enter restaurants from the front doors, sit at the heads of conference tables, run corporations and national nonprofits, own professional sports teams, lead higher learning institutions, own media empires, and dream beyond what was possible.

No words or deeds could ever thank them enough for facing situations they weren't sure they would make it out of. We should be forever grateful that they gave so much, even sacrificed a normal life, so that we could enjoy life as true American citizens and not second-class residents. I wanted to remind those leaders that their work had paved the way for Mr. Obama.

The distinction between old people and the elders is important to repeat because there are elders whose presence is critical for the work. We need their insight, their wisdom, and their experiences to help us move forward. My generation can't do it without the elders, and the elders can't do it without us. This is why I think it's critical to pay homage to those who have come before us. I've benefited from their sacrifices. I understand that, without them, I cannot be who I am today.

At the same time, I need some of the old folks to understand that we must get beyond dwelling in what happened in the past. I need some of the old folks to understand that the movement is not over. As long as there are more black men in the criminal justice system than in colleges and universities, as long as there remain disparities in health care and wealth creation, as long as there continue to be black-on-black crime, poverty in our communities, and an education system that leaves the poor and students of color behind—the "movement" continues. We need young, old, and the elders to stand together in today's movement.

The movement in the black community today is not always about Confederate flags and church burnings. It's no longer about ridding ourselves of Jim Crow. Today's movement is not about overcoming someday or seeking access to the ballot.

Today's movement is about the blood of black men who die at the hands of other black men. It's about overcoming the cycles of complacency and the arrogance of "I made it, why can't you?" Today's movement is facing the truth about the two enemies of will in the black community: continuing poverty because of the lack of opportunity and upward mobility, and *choosing* poverty because it's easier and faster to sell drugs to one another and a badge of honor to go to prison. Today's movement is about the scores of people who refuse to vote and make their voices heard in our process, regardless of their color or age. While racism in America is still alive and well, we have other issues that keep us away from opportunity and moving forward as well.

Imagine the difference we could make if we bridged this gap and could benefit from the wisdom of the elders and move forward with the insight of young folks. How significant it would be if the old folks told us the truth about their own experiences and struggles. How incredible it would be if the old folks would celebrate young people for taking on these challenges as they did when they were young, and if they shared their knowledge to make us better.

Dr. King was thirty-four years old when he led the march on Washington. He was just twenty-six when he headed the Montgomery Improvement Association, which led the successful 381-day Montgomery Bus Boycott. The old folks should remind themselves that they weren't the gray-haired, wise ones when they had the courage to go to jail and get beaten with billy clubs. We must speak to the old folks and help them understand the importance of sharing their stories—not as a badge of honor, but as a way to shed light on our strength. It's important for the older generation to share the mistakes and the lessons learned so that we won't repeat them. It's important to tell the truth that not everybody marched with Dr. King and not everybody was a proud member of the NAACP and SCLC.

Instead, they should tell the truth—that some folks were too scared, that their parents wouldn't let them participate, that some black folks just wanted to keep things like they were because they didn't want to rock the boat. They should share that we must think strategically, not tactically. Old folks should share how they handled the people who weren't willing to march. They have to share that the community meetings weren't always standing-room only. They have to share that there were moments where they couldn't get people mobilized and fired up. They have to share that there were moments when they felt scared and unprepared. They have to share that there were moments when they thought about giving up because the consequences were too grave.

They should talk about their spouses and children who wanted them home at night. They should tell us the things that brought them through, that kept them from giving up on the movement and themselves. They should tell us how great we are as a people and how, if we can get through slavery and Jim Crow, we can get through anything. They should make it a priority to help train the next generation of leaders so that we can build on their foundation and take the work to the next level. What could we do if our elders focused on succession planning, helped to prepare the next generation of leaders, and were intentional about making sure we were successful? If they shared their wisdom and helped prepare us to take the reins, I believe my generation would then show the respect that is deserved to those who sacrificed everything so that we could move forward as a nation.

> "A man who pays respect to the great paves
> the way for his own greatness."
> —African proverb

Young people have plenty to bring to the table and plenty to learn. You cannot employ only 1968 tactics in the technological age. At the same time, you cannot employ direct action tactics today without using the timeless lessons of having a strategy and understanding the problem and the opposition first. Rather than finding ways to be different, we need to find ways to work together. Rather than always asking whether there is still a need for the NAACP, Rainbow PUSH, and other organizations, let's join them and make them more relevant to the lives of the people who need them the most.

Rather than assuming the elders don't understand our plight in today's struggle, let's sit down and learn from the struggles of yesteryear. Let's find ways that we can work together and find things that we have in common. To deconstruct the beasts of inequality and injustice, we need all of us at the table. We can leave the egos, the attitudes, the arrogance, the two-way ageism, the sexism, and the negativity at the door. Otherwise, what good are the lessons we learned? What good is the work that we do separately? What good was the work that was done yesteryear if we can't build on the lessons we learned and the victories they earned to help us combat the many issues we deal with today?

This generation has a unique opportunity to bridge the gap. It was our parents and grandparents who lived through the civil rights movement, and it's our responsibility to share that knowledge and take what we've learned to make our communities better, to take what we know from our past to create a better future. We are the bridge. If we are ever to see our communities progressing, we have to be the bridge and close this gap. We want to learn how to keep getting up when the opposition keeps pushing us down. We want to learn how to keep fighting when the task seems too hard. Those lessons can teach us how to take on movements that seem too big. The elders can talk about organizing the few to help the masses. They can tell us about being David and taking on the Goliaths. Those lessons can help us navigate through the challenges of taking on the mediocrity of public education and the enemy that sometimes exists in our own ranks. Those lessons can inspire those who move through their lives with a feeling of nothingness. So many of us yearn for some older person to take us to the side and help us get back on course or create a new course.

As young people, we have to open our minds and hearts to wisdom. We have to be willing to couple our intellect and innovation of the twenty-first century with the wisdom and fire that existed in movements before us. We have to be willing to seek advice and be open to learning from past mistakes and victories. We can't count out the power of the tried-and-true strategies and tactics that have sparked and created successful movements around the country and the world.

Age eight in my baton twirling costume

My favorite picture with my mom, taken when I was in college.

With David on a date. To maintain a healthy relationship we have a weekly lunch and date regularly. No children and no cell phones!

With Reverend Dr. Joseph E. Lowery, the Dean of the Civil Rights movement and one of the most influential people in my life, along with his wife, Mrs. Evelyn Lowery, an activist and leader in her own right. This picture was taken in Atlanta at the Iowa Caucus watch party in 2008.

Picture with my parents Joseph and Wynell Thomas, my daughter
Lailah, my husband David before my brother Joey's wedding

Lailah was a year old. She's a girly girl all the way!

With my daughter Lailah (1) and my stepson
Rashaan (13) after Easter service 2009

I met then Senator Barack Obama two days
before having my daughter Lailah

With Georgia Governor Sonny Perdue at
my first bill signing in 2008

At the speaker's podium trying to lobby the former speaker
Glenn Richardson for my public school choice law HB251

Hosting the scholars from the all-girl Ivy Preparatory
Academy Charter school at the capitol

Hosting a group of young professionals during our annual Young
Professionals Day at the capitol, sponsored by my legislative office.

At the infamous well where we deliver speeches. This was taken
during the House debate on health care reform the day after the
historic health care reform bill passed in Congress in 2010

With students from my "Saturdays with My State Rep"
program. This is a leadership and personal development
program I run for high school students in my district.
This was taken after a community service project.

We have to be willing to ask for advice and mentorship. I remember feeling neglected and isolated when I got into the legislature. I was hoping that, similar to my life in high school and college, some woman was going to take me under her wing to share every lesson she had. I found myself resentful toward the women who didn't come to ask me if I needed help. I expected that they would know of my need because I was new. Those were my mistakes, and I should have asked. I should have understood that sometimes the gaps between generations are very wide, and the resentment that people carry around because of their own experiences can get in the way of them helping those coming behind them. We have to take down these walls that imply we know everything and start asking for help, advice, and counsel. We can learn intergenerationally and, as importantly, contribute because of our unique experiences and what we bring to the table.

This generation gap must be closed because there is too much work that has to be done in our community. We have too many battles to fight to get bogged down on age. There is enough work to do that we need all of us standing on the front lines. We can't do it alone.

Despite the lack of support from most members of the Congressional Black Caucus, older people in African American and Latino communities, and the status quo in the Democratic party, Obama won anyway. He teaches my generation a powerful lesson that, instead of waiting for the torch to be passed, sometimes you just have to snatch it. We can't wait for the tap, the permission, or the blessing. Many of us are talented, well-equipped, and ready to take the reins. We hesitate because we don't want to ruffle any feathers, and, like me, we were taught to "respect" our elders; so the thought of snatching the torch seems harsh. What's more harsh is the work that remains undone because old folks aren't ready to let go. They need something to feel significant, so, at times, they take up space that could be occupied by brighter minds and fresher insights.

The good news is that there are individuals and organizations, particularly in the younger generation, who do understand succession planning. While we could stay in positions for a lifetime, we choose not to—one, because there are other things we want to do with our lives; two, because we know that at some point it's important to introduce new ideas and insight to the new challenges that we face as a community. Being stagnant in a position means that you aren't willing to accept change, you can't see the world changing around you, and thus your perspective becomes outdated and many times of little use for the challenges you face.

I'm not saying to get rid of the elders. It's vital to have institutional memory—people who have been around to teach the process and provide some historical framework for how we got to this point. This is where you create the balance of old and new, each teaching the other something and maximizing on the strengths of both. Succession planning means that when the new come in, the old take them under their wings, show them the ropes, and share all their knowledge to prepare their successors to take it to the next level. It's how this country was created. The constitution was created by men whose world was drastically different from the world we have today. Each generation builds upon this foundation and contributes their experiences and insight to make us better.

Young people don't have to wait to be tapped to serve in the community, run for office, or lead in the capacity they are prepared to lead in. That means that we don't have to wait for permission or for the torch to be passed. As the old folks have reminded us on many occasions, there is no torch; and, if there ever was one, no one passed it to them. I say; if there is a torch, snatch it. Take hold of those things that you are passionate about and run on.

Too many of us grow up in organizations or in communities where we are waiting for someone to tell us that it's our turn, that we've paid our dues that someone is stepping out of the way. It's not going to happen. How often will anyone who holds power, prestige, or the pedestal willingly give it up? While we sit around waiting for the anointing, there are communities suffering. We cannot wait for our turn, for the degrees on the wall, the spouse, the picture-perfect life, or the perfect circumstances. We need to get up and get involved with the urgency of now.

❧ LESSONS I LEARNED ALONG THE WAY ❧

1. Never apologize for snatching the torch. To bridge the generational gap, we need elders and we need young people who are willing to work with each other. What we don't need are old folks. Rather than sitting around, waiting for an anointing or appointing from people who are too busy holding onto the past, rather than waiting for them to pass the torch, snatch it. Take hold of the mantle of leadership and stop waiting. There is work to be done in our communities, and we can't wait for someone to decide that he or she is ready to pass the torch.

2. Learn from the victories and failure of our forefathers. We should celebrate both the struggles and triumphs in our history. Those experiences have shaped who we are as a country and as a people. Dwelling on the failures without building upon those obstacles simply condemns us to repeat them.

3. Create your own succession planning. We should constantly think about who is coming behind us. Who can we help along our journey to keep them from facing the same challenges we faced? Whatever position we acquire, we simply cannot hold on to it forever. Find someone who can build on what you have created, because no one can take away from your legacy. Take the time to train someone to take your position. Pass down the knowledge and your experiences. Instill the values you want to see. Help pass the torch so we can create a better world than we found it.

4. Ask for mentorship. Sometimes we have no mentors because we haven't asked. Because we know there's a generation gap, we have to take it upon ourselves to create the relationships. Not everyone will want to mentor, but sometimes our elders don't know we want help, so don't be afraid to ask. Create a space where you are willing to listen to the insight of the elders, even if you don't accept all of their advice.

7. THE ONES WE'VE BEEN WAITING FOR

S O OFTEN, WE ARE CAUGHT up in the day-to-day of life. We go to work or school, we spend the day looking for a job, and we take care of our families. Sadly, most of us don't get involved in issues until they affect us directly. How many times have you been affected by something for the first time and realized that you wouldn't have known the severity of the issue had you not experienced it yourself? Sometimes, God allows things to happen to us so that we can feel what it's like, so that we won't judge others, and so that we can take action. Rather than wait for the most charismatic leader who can get everyone on their feet with moving oration, someone who will come and save the masses, someone who will soon come and have all the answers, consider that oftentimes the one you've been waiting for is you.

We can find all of the excuses in the world about how we want to get involved, but ... (fill in the blank). We make excuses for ourselves about why we can't get involved just yet. It reminds me of being in church. After the sermon, the preacher "opens the doors to the church."

Every Sunday we know the drill. We can almost time it to the minute. Whether the sermon is strong and moves hundreds, or a specific message that only touches a few, we know at some point that the doors will be opened. There are Sundays when there are numerous takers of the invitation and Sundays when no one goes. As the invitation is extended, I hear people whisper to their neighbors, "I'll wait until next Sunday." They say, "There are too many people up there," or "I don't want to be up there by myself." The preacher will remind us that tomorrow is not promised. It will move a few more, but some will stay where they are, convincing themselves that, although they know they want and need to take that step, they just want to wait a little bit longer.

I wish I could tell you to lean over and tap your neighbor and say, "What are you waiting for?" Instead, I'll ask you. What are you waiting for? There will never be a better time than now to advocate for those things that help an entire group of people. There is no better time to stand up for the children to get a quality education or the children in your state to stop being tried as adults. There is no better time to stand in the gap for those who need a bridge to a better tomorrow. There is no better time to get up now and do those things that you have been called to do. Stop waiting for the kids to get older, to get married, to finish school, to have enough degrees, to do this, to do that. We can spend all of our lives waiting to do something and end up never doing it because we were always waiting for tomorrow.

We have to stop waiting. We have to stop hoping that someone else is going to do it, even in our own lives. We want to better ourselves professionally and personally, yet, once we decide we want better, we spend the first six months pontificating about how much we want to change or grow. We get complacent, even lazy, about putting those things in place that get us closer to where we want to be. We get stuck in the rut, the endless cycle of complacency that tells us things should be the way they are. It tells us that what we want to do takes so much and we just don't have the resources to get it done.

We've been convinced that if we don't have a movement with thousands of people, then we can't make change. Because we don't fit in the same little package that we are used to seeing "leaders" in, we continue to think, "I want to do something about this issue, but I'm going to wait for the leader to come so I can follow. I'm not smart enough. I don't have it all together. I've made too many mistakes. I'm not ready to lead. It's easier to follow. I'm going to wait for a better time. I don't have enough people." Those are the things we tell ourselves.

Leadership and servant leadership in particular are not about waiting for all of the circumstances to be right or for everyone to come along with you with the same passion you have. Leadership is about seeing the need and filling that void. Leadership is a calling whether you are in politics, leading your team at work, or in your homeowner's association. Leadership requires us to get there first, leave last, manage attitudes, and balance the needs and schedules of other people—all, when you want results, with a smile.

Leadership succeeds when you can strike a good balance between creating a path where none exists and listening to the people around you when they may know another route. It is understanding your own strengths and weaknesses and having the right people around you that make you better. Leadership is staying when everyone else has gone home and figuring it out because you understand that it ultimately falls back on you.

Leadership can be isolating, even in a room of leaders. It's there that you understand the difference between a calling and a position. Positions give you the perks and even the responsibilities that come with leadership. Positions don't equip you with the moral compass and heart for the people you must serve. Leadership is also the ability to step out and be the first to speak up even when you are in the minority. Leadership is acceptance that not everyone will be a part of the movement and that it's the small number of people who do the work that benefits the masses. So often we get caught up on the fact that we have hundreds on the rolls but only a few who show up to the meetings. We get disheartened about the number of people who didn't come rather than utilizing the people who did. Focusing on the absent people only takes your eyes off the prize.

Leadership is challenging the status quo. It's requiring yourself and others to find a new or a better way to get something done. It is the wisdom to understand the past but not to rely on it—rather, to move forward. Leadership is the ability to make the tough decisions and not lose sleep worrying about the consequences. Leadership is the gut in you that forces you to move, because your conscience won't let you stay still. Leadership is accepting the blame and sharing the credit. It's staying on the cutting edge and constantly challenging yourself to be better. Leadership can make you feel lonely when there are plenty of other people around you.

Some of the most important lessons I've learned about leadership have come in the most difficult times. That seems to be when your leadership is most important. What you are able to do in the easy and comfortable times is less important than the decisions you make when things are difficult. Leadership is the ability to lead from your values rather than from expedience.

The fruits of leadership are in the eyes of those who walk with you. There are moments when you realize that your sacrifices were well worth it. It's the law that passed and the people whose lives it will change because of your leadership. It's the client who chooses your portfolio over the competition because of your willingness to go against the grain.

I had a hard leadership lesson one session when we were faced with a bill for a powerful company. Nearly all the legislators on both sides had strong relationships with that company. Every time we had community events, this company was there to support. Each time we wanted tickets to a sports event, they were right there to help us accommodate our friends and families. It wasn't about the money they were willing to spend but the relationships they had built with each one of us.

When the legislation came that would give them power beyond what the existing regulatory authority could give, it challenged the best of leaders in our assembly. I struggled with the decision on how to vote. It was an issue that I barely understood, and I knew that few of my constituents would be paying attention to it. In fact, many of them, including my own family, didn't even use this company, so it would have no impact on us. I danced with the idea of voting to help the company to maintain my relationship and keep the support coming. I thought of very good reasons why I could vote for it. I didn't want to make anyone mad, because their support helped me offer programs in my district.

I also thought about my goal to work in a more bi-partisan way and try to keep an open mind about business issues. This would have been a great opportunity to position myself as independent in thought and someone both sides could come to. I even talked with my staff about weighing the options for the greater good. We convinced one another that this was an opportunity to thank my lobbyist friends for always being there when I asked. It seemed pretty simple on the surface because I wasn't really considering the merits of the bill. When the easy seemed too easy, I had to take a step back. I hosted a town hall meeting on the issue, and, by the time it was over, those constituents present were very much opposed to this measure. Still I would have had the opportunity to vote in favor of this bill because, with only fifteen people present, I could argue that their views didn't represent the over forty-five thousand in my district. Still, I wanted to help my friends so that ultimately I could continue to help my community.

One thing I knew from the town hall is that more information was coming out that made the decision more difficult. There were valid arguments being made against this bill, and they were strong and sensible. Things weren't sitting comfortably with me then, and it became a very difficult decision for me. I called two friends, one political, one not, to talk through my decision and to weigh the benefits and consequences of each decision. Although they didn't know one another and both came with very different reasons, both suggested I simply avoid the vote.

In political terms, this is called walking on a vote. In some legislative bodies this would be voting present rather than yes or no on the measure. It's a way of saying, "I'm here, but I wish not to vote on this measure for whatever reason." In our body, voting present is not an option. In fact, we have a rule that if you are on the floor (meaning, in the chamber), you must cast a vote. To avoid casting a vote on some legislative matters, many of my colleagues "take a walk," meaning, they conveniently leave the chamber or get excused for the rest of the day so as not to go on record for or against a particular measure.

I have never purposely walked on a vote. There have been times when I have been off the floor talking to a constituent or lobbyist outside the chamber and missed votes, but I have never purposely walked out to avoid voting. I didn't really understand "walking" until this particular vote. It was the easiest thing to do. If I walked on the vote, I wouldn't have to vote yes and go against what my constituents and other political allies asked me to do, neither would I have to vote no and "bite the hand" that had helped support my community initiatives. This was one of those instances that teach us not to say what you won't do, because, until you are in that situation, you may not always react in the way you think.

The day before the vote, I found out that my grandfather was sick. He lived in Miami and it was serious, so my mother and I made plans to go and visit. I called my staff to let them know of my possible trip, and now, as they suggested, I had the perfect reason to miss the vote. Obviously, I would never use something as serious as an excuse, but this situation was the out some would say I needed. The more I thought about it, the more I agreed that this was my chance to avoid this vote and have no one mad at me.

The next morning as I was preparing to head to Miami, my mother and I worked on flights. I had a speaking engagement the next morning, so I knew I would be making a quick trip to Miami to ensure I was back for that. It turned out that I couldn't find a flight that fit my schedule, but I booked a ticket for my mother. While I was at home working on the ticket, I watched the House proceedings online. There were numerous bills to be voted on that day, but this day I knew would be pretty big because everyone knew this controversial bill would come for a vote. The debate started that morning, and I tuned in. By this time, the necessary parties knew that I was headed to Miami, so, in my mind; there was no need to head down to the capitol. In fact, I had even called my friend from the company to let him know I wouldn't be present that day and wished him well on the vote.

For hours my colleagues on both sides of the aisle (Democrat and Republican) made strong arguments for and against the bill. The most compelling came from those who cautioned the members of the House not to make this decision based on relationships with the lobbyists but based on the merits of the issue. Individuals from both parties spoke about standing on principle and voting their conscience. For a while I sat there watching like a spectator, reveling in the opportunity to skirt this issue. It was almost like going to a sports game and watching with bated breath to see which team would prevail in the end.

Finally, an hour or so of debate went by and I felt that stinging in my gut. It's what I always feel when it's time for me to take an unpopular stance. I've felt it since I was in middle school—that moment when you see someone being wronged, when everyone else is silent but the urge to act weighs heavily on your heart until you do. It's not until I take that action that my soul rests. I imagine it's what most servant leaders feel when they are standing for what they believe in the midst of a storm. It's that feeling that I've had all of my life that says I must move now.

Three hours into the debate, I decided that I did not need to use any excuse but that it was time for me to take a stand. I thought about the five interns in my office that session who were learning about the political process through my lens. I wanted them to learn how to follow a bill through the process and help me organize my Lobby Days at the capitol. I also wanted them to learn what service in action looked like. I wanted them to see their representative act in the best interest of their constituents, not because of programs, but because of their wishes. I didn't want them to internalize the ongoing cycle of politics at its worst when "politicians" make decisions based on external factors that have very little to do with merit. I wanted them to walk away from the experience in my office learning the importance of constituent feedback and trusting that when you do the right thing for constituents, support for the programs and initiatives will come without having to compromise your own values and beliefs. I wanted them to see what real leadership looked like. At that moment, I was learning what it looked like for myself.

I got dressed and rushed down to the capitol. I didn't know if my vote would make a difference on the outcome of the measure, but I knew I needed to cast my vote. By the time I got to the capitol, the debate was still going on. By the time I signed in and listened to two more speakers, it was time for the vote. I also called my lobbyist friend to let him know that I did make it for the vote after all and gave him the heads up on how I would vote. That heavy burden I felt like I'd been carrying over those last few days suddenly felt lighter. The speaker ordered voting machines opened, and I voted *no*. I voted no because I realized at the end of the day that my desire to vote in favor of the bill had not been rooted in principle or merit. It had been based on my relationships and trying to convince myself that I didn't want to lose friends or support from this company for my programs. For a second, I had been willing to ignore the compelling arguments against the bill because of relationships.

Not once during my entire tenure in the legislature had I attempted to make what I consider a "political" decision. Now, for the first time, I not only understood how my colleagues could make such decisions in the past, but for a brief moment, I realized that I was willing to do it, too. It was one of the most critical moments in my legislative tenure and one of the most powerful lessons I learned in life. In that moment, my principles and my own rhetoric were tested. I always talked about not becoming a part of the institution but, instead, being the change I wanted to see in a system that seemed so broken. When it came to deciding how to vote on the Confederate flag or gay marriage, people often commented on my courage and willingness to stand up for my beliefs. The truth is, those weren't acts of courage because I had no conflict. There was no question about where I would stand on issues of justice and equality.

I learned that day that leadership is not only voting my conscience but it's exercising courage when you feel torn. Leadership means thinking about the impact of your decisions on the people who look to you as a leader. Leadership is not discounting the voices of the minority because you didn't hear from the majority. Leadership is taking a stand even when you don't have to. I could have easily stayed at home that day and allowed that vote to happen without me. The truth is, the bill would have passed anyway, and no one would have blamed me for missing the vote. In fact, I would venture to say that very few people would have cared. Leadership is not about what people see or notice. It's not about whether your voice makes the majority. Leadership is who you are when no one is looking. Leadership is about standing on principle when no one is making you. Leadership is doing the right thing, even when there are consequences.

❖ Lessons I Learned Along the Way ❖

1. Never apologize for leading. Sometimes we think it's easier to sit back and let someone else lead. When you are called to lead, it's up to you to step up to the plate. Everyone may not always agree. Everyone may not always understand. Leadership is about who you are and what you've been called to do. Don't hang up the phone.

2. Don't be afraid if you don't have all the answers. Leadership isn't about having all of the answers. It is about having the wisdom to know what you don't know and seeking the answers. Never be afraid to listen to the people you are leading.

3. Surround yourself with the right people. As leaders, we must surround ourselves with people who will tell us the truth about ourselves, offer wise counsel, and support us even when we don't take their advice. Surrounding ourselves with good people ensures that we are never alone and that we always have people around who can balance our weaknesses with their strengths.

4. Hold yourself accountable first. Leadership is about holding yourself accountable, not about who is watching. It's about the core of who you are and what makes you a leader in the first place.

5. Always strive to make yourself better. True leaders are constantly looking for opportunities to grow. Read. Listen to inspiring messages. Pour positive things and more knowledge into yourself so that you grow and become better each day. Never become comfortable with where you are. Stretch yourself. Challenge yourself to be the very best you can be. Don't stop until your best becomes better.

8. Faith Got Me Through

AFTER EIGHT YEARS IN THE legislature and over thirty-one years on this earth, it seems like I've gone through so much. Whether it was the residency challenge that could have ended my so-called political career, challenging the speaker of the house and being threatened with censure, or, more important than all of that, trying to get pregnant and not knowing if my marriage would work out after all David and I had been through, there was only one way I could have made it through. It was my faith.

We often hear sermons about the importance of faith and can refer to the Scripture that says all we need is faith the size of a mustard seed. I will admit I have different levels of faith in all of these situations. What remained constant was my belief that, if I could get through the residency challenge and God could work that out, certainly He could work out the other issues that I faced after that. I have also developed the ability to remain calm in the midst of storms. How? Having life experiences and seeing how I got through them all remind me that nothing is too hard for God.

Sometimes we have to go through those drills in our minds, because things happen and one particularly difficult situation tends to cloud our minds and thoughts about our entire reality. What you realize is that if you just step back and trust God, things will happen in His time and in His way. When we try to maneuver and make things happen on our own, we quickly find that we don't get very far. This is not to say that we don't have work to do. We absolutely have our parts to play. There are times when we have done everything we can possibly do, and then we have to just trust our way through a situation.

When I was in the midst of my residency challenge, there were so many people along the way who talked about the impossibilities. They talked about the law and the other people before me who had faced the same challenges. When we lost the first case, the chances were even slimmer. The calls started coming in even more. People around me were afraid for me and what the outcome would be. There were times when I was unsure. I didn't know how we could win this. I did believe in my heart, though, that God had brought us too far to turn back. We had endorsements by the key political action committees like the women's group, labor, and organizations; there was excitement in the district.

We were changing how politics was done in Cobb County, and I knew in my heart of hearts that this was all happening for a reason. That reason didn't have to be that we were going to be successful. It very well could have meant that politics wasn't for me. Maybe I was setting the foundation for someone else. It could have been the start of new activism in Cobb County and this was the way God was bringing us together. I didn't know what it meant, but I knew it was all for a reason and somehow it would work out.

My lawyer, Brian Spears, who is the best at these types of cases, had been down this road many times. He found the best case for precedence he could. He gave my case the best legal skill possible. Even he had a little doubt about how this case would turn out. That was his job—to tell me the truth and provide his legal opinion on what the end result would be. It was my job as a woman of faith to believe beyond all impossibilities and to put my faith, not in my lawyer or even the judge, but in God who is the creator of all things. I remember my lawyer saying he didn't know how this would turn out or even how we could win. I recall saying to myself, *I do.*

And we did. When that judge overturned the decision and determined that faxing the challenge was not appropriate, I knew it was only God. I didn't know the decision would turn out in my favor, but I believed the situation would. Of all of the challenges I have faced in my life that was the one that taught me most about faith. It's the situation that I refer to in speeches to encourage others, but it's also the one that I refer to whenever I face new challenges in my life. It is how I remind myself that God can do anything. It's how I remind myself to remain patient and trust that somehow, some way, God is going to work this out.

That was the lesson I recalled in my darkest moments after I challenged the speaker. I would walk into the chamber and my colleagues were afraid to speak to me. I was the ostracized member that some wouldn't even look at. I felt alone and abandoned, even by people who were supposed to be my mentors. I knew that people were talking about me behind my back. I knew that I lost friends or people I thought were friends. I also knew that the media was watching every step that I would take.

What made things worse was that I felt like there was no one I could turn to who could help me get through that period. There was no one I could call who could understand the darkness of that hour, no one that I could call and ask what to do next, because very few people could understand the position that I was in and the consequences that were to come as a result of what I had done. Of course, there were people outside of the chamber who were proud of me. I remember walking into that People's Agenda meeting and people giving me a standing ovation. I was humbled by that moment, but still no one could understand the pain I felt by being shunned by the people I was elected to serve with. At the time, the pats on the back, the words of encouragement, could not fill the void in my heart.

Finally, I had to remember the faith that had gotten me through the residency challenge. I had to recall what it felt like to be on the front page of the local paper, face going to court and still work to get votes. I had to recall the strength that it took to go and knock on doors and ask for votes when my name wasn't even on the ballot, the courage that it took to look voters in the eyes and ask for their vote, to ask them to trust me that it would all work out. I remembered how so many people said it was impossible for us to win and how we should just give up. I remembered those moments, and I had to encourage myself to stand strong on my convictions. I recalled how it wasn't my lawyer or even the judge who had brought me through that situation; it was God.

It was God who had helped me get to Election Day with a victory, and it was God who would stand with me through that dark hour in the legislature. It was God who sent the lobbyist in the halls to tell me not to apologize and to wear that censure like a badge of honor. It was God who spoke to my spirit and said, "Stand still on my convictions." It was my faith that told me God was with me at that moment and would stand with me when my colleagues wouldn't come around. And He did. Many of the same colleagues who were sent to me in private to get me to apologize now laud me in public for my courage and convictions to speak truth to power. I couldn't understand then why I would have to go through something like this. I didn't understand why it had to be me. I didn't understand, at the time, what the silver lining was or what could possibly come out of this that would help me in the future.

There are still consequences that I face in the world of politics because of that day in 2005. I am still trying to build and rebuild relationships. Some of my colleagues still see that incident before they see me. The lessons I learned during that time about myself, my abilities, my courage, and my resilience; the people I discovered who are my true friends and allies; the people in the community who developed a new respect for me; the lessons I learned about the importance of standing on principle—these are all things I could not have learned if it were not for March 12, 2005. Frederick Douglass said, "Without struggle there is no progress."

Progress was not just the Morgan switch. Progress was also the change in how business was done, because now there was a brighter light shining on the environment we were serving in. Progress involved the people who galvanized to support me. Progress was Dr. Lowery showing up at the speaker's office and defending the principles on which I stood. Progress was the new respect my colleagues found, once they realized the community response to my actions. For me, the most important progress was the reassurance I felt that I was doing the right thing and the conviction I now feel for never apologizing for who I am.

God will sometimes allow things to happen in our lives for a few reasons. One, He wants to remind us that He is in control. Sometimes He has to put us in situations where our backs are against the wall and there seems to be no way to get out. In real life terms, there most likely *is* no way to get out. He shows us that we can amass all of the material things and the great jobs, the nice families, and all of the things we believe we are supposed to have. Sometimes when we acquire all of those things, we start believing that it's because of our talents and our great skill. Every once in a while I believe God will put us in situations to remind us that it's not because of us or the people around us. Sure, those people helped and were sent by Him. There are times when we have to be reminded that we need God. Without Him we can't have all of the things we were destined to have. I also believe that God puts us in these situations to sharpen our faith. Sometimes it's to prepare us for what is coming ahead. We have to prove to ourselves that we can get through these smaller situations so that we can overcome the big ones that will come our way.

We have all heard the phrases: "Sometimes you have to go through a setback to get through a come up" or "God is giving you a test for your testimony." Whatever the phrase you subscribe to, I believe it. I believe that when God has placed something in your heart to do, to work on, to create, He also allows for certain obstacles to come in your way. Rather than seeing it as a sign that it isn't what you are supposed to do, sometimes it's simply preparation for the real challenges you will face when you get there. Without faith, you can be easily shaken. If you aren't ready for the small challenges, how are you going to be ready for the real stuff when it comes?

Consider all of the people we admire and look up to. We admire them because of their accomplishments, and we admire them for the mountains they had to climb to get there. Their stories of triumph are what help their successes mean even more to us. This doesn't mean that life is just about adversity and things can't be easy. It just means that there are moments when we are tested and our faith is tested. There are moments when we are allowed to go through certain things so that we can help other people along the way. It means that sometimes we are allowed to face these challenges so we have greater appreciation for how good God is and how awesome things can be when we rely on our faith and not solely on our own talents and relationships.

Are you going through something difficult right now? Have you given up? Have you given up on your passion because you decided it was too hard? Perhaps the road has yet to be paved and you don't think you have the energy to create the path for yourself. What is it that you have been called to do but you won't do? Is it because you are afraid of what comes next? What is it that God says to do, but *you* say you can't because you aren't qualified or you don't have the time or the relationships to make it happen? What have you let go because you were afraid of the challenges ahead? It's time for you to recall the other situations in your life when you thought you weren't going to make it. You are still here, aren't you? What makes you think that, if you got through those other times, you can't get through this one? It's time to check your faith.

❖ LESSONS I LEARNED ALONG THE WAY ❖

1. Trust that whatever the circumstances, it has already been worked out. You may not understand how, when, or who will help make it happen. Just trust that God is bigger than all of us and always has a plan for your life. Many times we have to learn lessons that will prepare us for bigger challenges we will face. Without that experience, we wouldn't have something to refer to. The challenge for each of us is not to get caught up in how big our problem is or how difficult it seems.

2. Never rely on the validation of other people. When you believe strongly about something, you cannot allow yourself to be shaken by the bad advice or the lack of faith of other people. They didn't give you that dream. People don't always understand who you are or who God made you to be. You know in your gut when you have been called to do something. It's not always the easiest thing to accomplish, and the road may not always be paved. If God intended for someone else to do it, He would have given it to them.

3. What is for you is for you. Sometimes God places dreams in our minds or spirits, and we start moving in that direction. When the going gets rough, we become discouraged and start second-guessing our own talents, or we question whether it was really God speaking to us. You must always remind yourself that what is for you is for you. It doesn't matter what it looks like to the human eye. It doesn't matter how bad it gets. What is for you is for you. No man, no problem, no situation can keep you from it.

Yes, those things may make your dream harder to get to or make you question the possibility. Always remember that nothing is too hard for God, and He will always give you those things that belong to you when you need them. When your faith is strong, you are more likely to take things in stride. People should be able to look at you and not know that things aren't going well. Why? Because we know that somehow it always works out. We should know that there's always some person or some solution that God will send our way. When you worry, you are telling God that you've forgotten He's in control. Let go, and let Him handle it. Do your part and He will do His.

4. Encourage yourself. There is a song that says, sometimes you have to encourage yourself. When we are in challenging times, we don't always have a friend we can call right there to help us feel better. Sometimes people don't understand your struggle. Remember when the people along the way couldn't encourage you because they had little or no faith of their own? Remember how you felt when you got through that situation and you came out better? That's what you should remember. When you find yourself in a new situation and it seems like your world is falling apart, recall that time when you made it through. Remind yourself that, if you made it through that situation, you can get through this one and you will. Encourage yourself. Be your own cheerleader. Become your own inspiration. Tape an inspirational quote on your wall or leave a powerful Scripture in your car. Do the things you have to do to encourage yourself.

5. Never underestimate the power of prayer and meditation. Sometimes we get so caught up in our situations that we forget who is in control. Stop and take time to breathe and talk to God or whoever your higher power is. I believe that our faith is strengthened when we take our problem to God and remind ourselves that He is really in control. You certainly can do your part, but going in prayer also reminds us that someone or something else has the final decision. Prayer and meditation is also calming. Go into a quiet space and let go.

9. A BLESSING AND A BURDEN

WHAT WE KNOW ABOUT HARDSHIPS in our lives is that they don't come based on color, gender, how much money we have, or our age. The older or younger you are doesn't determine the degree of challenges we face in our lives. If you were to study movements around the world, the one common denominator is the role young people have played in challenging the status quo and pushing for change despite the objections of the establishment. I find myself frustrated, though, that this fact is rarely celebrated or acknowledged. We forget that it's young people who have the courage, the ability to think outside the box, and the ability to add a fresh perspective, particularly in the legislative and political processes.

Rather than being celebrated for our courage and sought after to add new insight to solving our nation's problems, we are instead often disregarded and second-guessed. I know it isn't just my experience. It happens to many of my colleagues around the country who share that youth seems to be a blessing and a curse. I know this because some of my work enables me to communicate regularly with young elected officials around the country.

We laugh and swap stories about all of the crazy things we hear our colleagues say. "I have a tie older than you," "My granddaughter is your age," "You are like one of my children," "Oh, I didn't know you were the representative; I thought you were the intern." What's not funny is being elected, coming to serve in our respective bodies, and having yet one more area in which we have to prove ourselves and our abilities to our colleagues—simply because of our youth.

The experience we had in Alabama when wanting to take what we thought was our rightful place at the front of the march still stings. But those kinds of experiences didn't stop there. Being elected has only shown me more of that. It's also shown me the lack of respect that exists for young people and the undervaluing of youth in our community as a whole. Even those who were young during the civil rights movement tend to forget what it took to face water hoses and dogs. Much like the high school and college students who were fearless in facing the police batons and jail, young people in this legislative process are fearless as well, and we are willing to take risks. If we don't, then it's easier for us to become a part of this status quo and just maintain what's been happening for decades.

Many people assume that my race or gender are the largest barriers in serving. I find it's my age. Anytime I would stand up on an issue, speak truth to power, or do anything that is considered going against the grain, like clockwork someone would be headed over to inform me that once I got older I would understand that I couldn't do those things or say those things. Ironically, there would always be someone outside the chamber who undoubtedly would come and thank me for standing up and for being different from most of my colleagues. They thanked me for having the courage to speak truth to power and wished they were like that when they were my age. A truly frustrating paradox is how there is one set of views on the "inside," but on the "outside," where everyday people are affected by our decisions, they are much more appreciative of a voice that speaks for them. This creates a strong support system in the community, around the state, and even around the country.

People are looking for elected officials who are willing take a stand and say things that aren't so popular, not just for the sake of speaking out or creating controversy, but to make change. It's my training in the NAACP, it's my upbringing where my parents taught me to speak up and help other people. It is who I am, and, quite frankly, that's who I will continue to be. It's not just the age difference, but my willingness to use my voice that makes me stick out so much in the legislature. Some of my colleagues want to say those same things; I know, because they say them in meetings. Either they don't have the courage or they fear the consequences that come with speaking truth to power, so they choose to be silent.

I recall my first session, when I faced the Sons of Confederate Veterans in my district. They asked me to attend a meeting to talk about my stance on the Confederate flag. I did, not without a little help from the Georgia Bureau of Investigation. One of my colleagues made the recommendation that I ask them to join me at the meeting, and I took the advice. When I arrived at the community center (where I now hold most of my town hall meetings), I was greeted with life-size Confederate flags all over the parking lot. I walked into the room and it was filled with older white men who stared and whispered to one another. The gathering consisted of these men, a few people I had brought with me, and camera crews from the local news stations. The meeting quickly began with their pledge of allegiance to the Confederate flag, their singing of their favorite anthem, "Dixie," and a session of letter-reading from the war. I was flabbergasted at best, as I feared what would come next.

After all that I had to endure prior to my part in the program, I was then introduced and began the "discussion" about the Confederate flag, specifically the battle emblem and how it can be seen in many pictures of hangings of black men. A discussion ensued, but eventually it got off track. They began degrading the NAACP. Their words got angrier and more hateful. It's the feeling you get as an American when someone spits on our flag. I felt overwhelmed by this reveling in the Confederacy and the hatred.

I decided at that moment that this meeting was a waste of my time and theirs. It was prompted by the flags everywhere, the singing of "Dixie," and the complete ignorance of how this flag was so disrespectful to black people in America. I was fed up. I knew at that moment that it could only get worse. There was a reason my colleague had advised me to take the GBI with me. I made a tough decision to stand up for myself. I stood up and walked out of that meeting. The news cameras followed me, along with the people who had attended the meeting with me—my husband, pastor, and a few others. We walked into the parking lot like we had escaped a lynching. Finally, the ordeal was over.

I didn't know how that experience would play to the public. The headlines in the newspapers described my walking out. The cameras played that part as well. The next day, I was swamped with e-mail from all over the country and many words of encouragement—through phone calls and frequent visits by complete strangers in the halls of the legislature. I also got a few hate e-mails calling me everything in the book. For the most part, people were proud of me and my courage to attend the meeting in the first place. I still don't regret going to the meeting.

Sometimes I do regret that I had to leave. Some of the editorials in the newspapers, days after, admonished me for walking out, citing my age as the reason. They noted that I would one day mature and stay at such a meeting to endure those conditions. Others saw it as standing up to the organization by even attending the meeting, and as not allowing myself to be disrespected by leaving. Once again, many of my colleagues, who had not had a chance to get to know me yet, began making their assumptions. They figured I was too young and just there to make headlines, not really serious about lawmaking.

Whether it was the moment after I walked out of the Sons of Confederate Veteran's meeting or the time I was being pressured to make a public apology to the speaker about refusing to relinquish the well, I found myself in a unique position. I had no one to turn to who knew exactly what I was experiencing and how to deal with it. Now, I do have somewhere to turn.

In 2005, I helped Tallahassee City Commissioner Andrew Gillum bring his dream to fruition, and together we created the Young Elected Officials Network. We have over five hundred young electeds around the country who may not share my exact experiences but who certainly understand what it means to be the youngest in the room. They know what it's like to be constantly questioned about your qualifications or to be mistaken for an intern or staffer rather than the elected official. They understand the battles we fight to prove our value, and we share advice on the process it takes to earn the respect of our colleagues. This group of people can understand the ridiculous comments that colleagues make—comments like the one someone made to me when I was pregnant with Lailah.

It was the first week of session, and the surprise of my pregnancy was settling down. Then one colleague walked up to me and said, "Alisha, I knew you were married, but I didn't realize that you were actually having sex." Of course, this was a poor attempt at a joke. I doubt if this would have been said to a middle-aged woman. In fact, an older woman probably would have slapped him for saying it. His comment was meant to be funny, as most of the comments were, but, unfortunately, it speaks more about the need for more young people in these kinds of spaces so their presence is not such a rarity.

Being pregnant throughout a session provided some benefit to me. For the first time, there were a lot of Republican men in particular who seemed to take much more of an interest in me. They were eager to share stories about their grandchildren and about their own families. I found it to be helpful that they saw me as a mother, someone "normal" they could relate to. I think that, before I was pregnant and other than being married, they didn't think they had much in common with me. I also believe that they did what most people do when a pregnant woman is around: they pay more attention. These guys were more accommodating and attentive and were happy to help me in any way that they could. I developed relationships with some of them that I would not otherwise have developed.

That wasn't the case in the black caucus. That was the same year that I ran for chairman of the group, and I can't help but believe that the men in the caucus had a harder time voting for me because they weren't sure I could handle the job while being with child. Of course, there were some who also were afraid of what I might say, or how much I would change things. Either way, it seemed that their decision not to vote for me (especially compared to the other candidates who were running) was based on my age, my style of leadership, or being pregnant.

Whatever the reason, it would have been nice to be judged among my peers in the black caucus based on my abilities and vision, rather than on the shortsightedness from which they made their decisions. Ironically, I ran for vice chair two years later, made it in a runoff, and lost by two votes in an election where more votes were cast than there were people in the room. The details are not worth explaining. I've learned from that experience to utilize my leadership abilities elsewhere. No love lost at all.

Sometimes, we have to learn how to use youth to our advantage. When I was running the first time and had just made it over the residency challenge, one of my opponents decided he was going to try to use the residency issue in a debate. In that particular debate, I was doing incredibly well. It was clear from my answers that I was much more connected to the community than my opponents were. If there had been a winner that night, I was definitely it. When Andy Bush got the opportunity to take a stab at sinking me, he commented on how long I'd lived in the district. In my quick wit, which didn't get me in trouble that time, I shot back, "I'm only twenty-three. I haven't lived anywhere for a long time." People in the audience smiled and some applauded. I was celebrating inside because that time my youth was my asset. In that debate I got to prove that it wasn't about age, it was about experience.

The beauty of being young is about the experiences we have that add perspective; it's about the energy we have to tackle a challenge. The value of youth in general is that where we sometimes lack life experience, we make up for it with the naiveté that anything is possible. We dream bigger dreams, because we have had less experiences and people in our lives to tell us we can't. We are willing to try new things, because we don't always know what works. I knew people were telling me a win wasn't possible. When we first got started, the impossibility of it all never crossed my mind or the minds of many of the young people who were on my campaign team. The beauty of not knowing limits and impossibilities is fascinating. How many things in our lives have we decided not to do because someone convinced us that it had been tried before and it just couldn't be done?

It's the same beauty that we see in babies. I used to watch my own daughter try to go down the stairs by herself. As her parents, David and I would tell her what she could and could not do. In the same way, people tell us we can't do things because some of them want to protect us from getting hurt, physically and emotionally. I understand it, and I don't get upset with people when they try to tell me how hard something will be. It's not so much about what they say; it's really about what you *do* with that information. It's really about how much we limit our own lives because we have convinced ourselves that there are limits in place and we have to stay within them.

It's not just about the courage that young people possess. It's also about what young people can see that older folks can't. Jamal Simmons, a Morehouse brother and friend in politics, once gave a great analogy. He said that not only should we value the shoulders we stand on as young people, but older people should value us standing on their shoulders. When a child sits on the shoulders of his or parent, he or she can see things up high that the adult can't see. Using the foundation on which we stand, we can see further ahead. What are the lessons that young people can teach and tell others about because of the view that they have? The vision and willingness that young people have to go through uncharted waters has created change and movements all around the world. There is strength in having vision. You can see the things that other people can't see.

There were many people who told Barack Obama that he should wait his turn and that the country wasn't ready to elect a black president. I'm sure there were many people he came across who warned him of all of the obstacles that would be in his way. Many of them had real life experiences that qualified them to give such advice. Thank God he didn't listen. If he didn't, why should you? We need to learn the lesson from young people who teach us to dare to dream, to forget about all of the "why we cant's" and think about how we *can* make it happen. There is real value in not focusing on the "why not" or dwelling on how hard something will be or the fact that it's never been done before.

Despite young people always standing on the front lines of every movement, our contributions can often get overlooked. That doesn't mean we should stop what we do. The goal is not to get the accolades; it's to get the job done. Despite not getting the acceptance at the level we want, we can't be discouraged. Now that I've served for a while, I can see the difference in how people treat me or look to me for my insight on a particular issue. Although age is still a challenge for me among my colleagues, I notice it gets better as each year goes by.

I think the most important thing to do when you are the youngest person in your job, whether it's in politics or not, is to continue to do your absolute best and carry yourself as such. Much like being the only person of color or only woman in a job, you feel like you have to prove yourself and be two times better than your colleagues. I would say that's true. It's not fair, and we don't like it; but that's the reality.

Second, I would encourage you to decide what one or two things you can focus on and become an expert in. Learn your craft so well that people have to come and talk to you about it. Become the go-to person on a specific project or skill set. It's what you should always do in a work situation, but it's especially important when you are young. In my case it's a set of issues. I'm focusing a great deal on education. Before that it was juvenile and criminal justice. Once people see that you are good at what you do, you work hard, and you are always prepared, they begin to focus more on that rather than your age. They never forget about your age, but it gives them something more to look at. I find that when education bills come up, many of my colleagues will ask me to explain it or make recommendations on how to vote. It's a great feeling to see when people trust my knowledge and insight and can get their minds off how young I am.

Third, proving yourself to your older colleagues won't happen overnight. I hate the fact that I have to be better than most and have to prove myself—and I still don't get treated with the same respect as other colleagues. But it's reality. It's how society treats youth, and until that changes, we have to be patient and accept that it's not our issue; it's theirs. I find that once you earn their respect, you finally get treated differently. I know it's hard, but, if you are dealing with this problem, I encourage you to keep pushing. Keep working hard, being the best at your craft, and earning the respect you are due. In the midst of it all, don't apologize for who you are—for being young, having new ideas and fresh insights, or being different. You have great value and should take your rightful place, whether you are given permission or not.

❖ Lessons I Learned Along the Way ❖

1. Never apologize for being young. As young people have always been on the frontlines of every movement, we are needed on the frontlines now. Don't apologize for being young, for seeing beyond what is in front of you, or for having nontraditional ideas. Never ask for permission to walk in your destiny. Be who you are, and be confident in the things you bring to the table, regardless of your age.

2. Don't let age keep you from hearing what young people have to say. We have all heard the expression, "Out of the mouth of babes." No one has all of the answers, but young people can add real value. Try to hear what the younger person is saying rather than discounting him or her as being inferior because they are young. Let's find ways to learn from one another.

3. If you don't see a space for yourself, create one. Sometimes, the effort to hold on to what is most familiar and how things have been for decades can shut young, energetic people out of entire institutions. If people are not willing to share information or create space for you in their institutions, create space for yourself. You have the ability to do the work necessary to prepare yourself. Don't allow conventional wisdom to determine your path.

4. Be patient. With time and hard work, your colleagues will respect you for who you are and what you bring to the table. It takes time, but it's worth it. Don't get caught up in their issues; keep your eyes on the prize. There isn't an easy or short-term fix, but keep working hard and you can do it.

5. Create a niche and work hard at perfecting your craft. Anyone who is in a professional environment should strive to be the best at what they do. The important thing to remember is that we cannot be experts in every area. Instead, find something that you enjoy, something that no one or very few people focus on, and become an expert in that area. Not only does it help you in the work that you are doing, but it also puts you in a unique place to be needed for your skill set. This is especially important for young people so that you can earn respect among your colleagues. You will be pleasantly surprised when you become the go-to person.

6. Work hard. Everyone knows that hard work pays off. If ageism is an issue for you, you have to give people the opportunity to focus on your work and not your age. Whether we like it or not, when you are the youngest person in your line of work, you represent all young people and have to prove that we have the ability, skill-set, and expertise to do the job and do it well. Represent us well.

7. Create a network. There is nothing like having a support system around you to share best practices, experiences, resources, and advice. I'm so grateful for Commissioner Gillum and his vision to create the YEO Network. Because of it, hundreds of elected young people who are courageous and progressive have a safe space. We all need that. If you don't have a network to turn to for support in your work, create one!

8. Value the contributions of older people. Young people know what it's like to be undervalued and disregarded because of our age. Let's not repeat that same ageism against older people. Let's value the many life experiences, sacrifices, and wisdom of people who want to share and help us grow. Realize that each of us has something we can bring to the table. Ideas and progress don't have an age on them.

10. Broke Activism

Activism, in my mind, is the act of advocating for an individual or a group of people to ensure their rights. The more well-known acts of activists are protests, marches, and rallies. I believe that activism is not just about rallying but organizing. It's organizing people to create change. You can organize them through e-mail campaigns, a petition, and even by coordinating meetings with decision-makers. I think most of us have a degree of activism in us where we see injustice and we are immediately ready to act. That is activism.

Sometimes the examples we see on television or in other forms of media are a bit extreme, and the activists are portrayed as abnormal and downright crazy. One criticism that is often given by young people to old folks is that a person has to choose between being a financially broke activist and being a silent part of the established system. As much as we know in our hearts that it's better to choose to stand up for what you believe in and advocate for those who have no voice, we see too many examples of old folks who spend their entire lives fighting for good causes who have very little in terms of financial stability.

At one extreme, it seems that the stronger your advocacy, the poorer you should be. When we look at some of our most prominent civil rights leaders, most of them were not wealthy people. In fact, many of them were struggling to make ends meet, and you could imagine the arguments with their families because they spent so much time working for free. Who was going to pay you to go to jail or picket? These were volunteer acts by people who put the causes before their own financial stability and family.

Criticizing this choice would be foolish and ungrateful. If it were not for their sacrifices, we know we wouldn't be where we are today as a nation and world. On the other hand, it's unrealistic to encourage young people to take on activism when they are watching the fate of elders who have given their entire lives to organizations and causes. When these activists die, we are taking up a collection to cover their expenses or help their families get by. I've watched organizations take advantage of individuals who started out when they were teenagers in the movement. They are now old and gray, and there was nothing created in the organization to help with insurance or retirement or any future planning.

I don't believe these organizations did this on purpose. I believe that they were all caught up in the movement and fighting for other people, and they never took the time to make sure their own futures were taken care of. Yes, these were noble actions, but these individuals were also ill-equipped to support their families or life after the movement. With the tools that young people have today and the many examples we can learn from about adequately preparing for out futures, we can't convince young people to take on a life of activism when the examples they see—accurate or not—are people who can only ask others for resources because they don't have any to give.

At the other extreme are activists who use certain causes to make money. Our leaders who are on the national stage are often accused of that. The perception is that they create problems or choose which battles they will fight based on the paycheck at the end. The criticism is that they threaten corporations with pickets and protests if they don't receive hush money or large contributions for their organizations . Sometimes, the perception is that these individuals thrive on certain communities that stay at the bottom of the totem pole in education, wealth, access, health, and any other big issue—because this keeps them working. The stereotype is that these are "poverty pimps." Negative statistics are emphasized to create a permanent job and thus a permanent stage for the activist to "speak" on the community's behalf. I'm not convinced that any of these conditions account for all of the activists we see.

I have had no financial dealings with any of these individuals to confirm or deny such allegations. I do know that we should consider what we deem as jobs, careers, or calling. Should we be able to get compensated for our work, even in the areas of public service? Shouldn't those who are sacrificing everything they have for us—even including their lives—have the ability to earn a living and take care of their families as well? Are we perpetuating the belief that in order to do civil rights work, you should remain poor? Are we simply "hating" on those national leaders who make a living at being an activist? What would be the difference between a civil rights activist and a pastor?

There is a rift even among preachers. The so-called prosperity preachers—whose churches have memberships in the thousands—may own several houses, cars, and even a jet. They argue that God wants us to be prosperous, while there is another school of thought that says preachers should be poor. Wherever we stand, we should challenge our own and our society's thinking when it says that those who do public service, whatever it is, should be paid less. Teachers, social workers, counselors, and others who spend their time helping people are the lowest paid on a professional scale. There are judges handing down decisions, who oftentimes earn a a fraction of what the lawyers who come before them earn. How do we shift our paradigm so that we aren't using up those people who sacrifice their own financial well-being for our collective benefit? How do we stop leaving these people with little financial wherewithal to show for their efforts? How do we encourage our organizations to fight just as hard for the people who work for them as they do for the rest of us?

If we are to get more young people involved in any movement, we have to begin to recreate the models. Otherwise we end up with a generation of young people who are completely disconnected and others who stay as far away as possible from the movement because they don't want to be marginalized or broke. This is the generation that can reach the world through their fingertips. We live in an "everything now" society, and all of the images around us tell us that if we work it right, we can have it now. With that kind of environment, who would choose a life that is noble yet lacks wealth and access to the things we want? This is not to say that we are all about material things. It means that we like acquiring our items of choice, want to appropriately provide for our families, and have the right and responsibility to do so.

That's why there is such a difference between the elders and old folks who are in the movement, and the young people who are in the movement. Make no mistake; there are thousands of young people across the country who are already on the front lines.

They are fighting issues like the Jena Six in Louisiana. Although some of our national leaders and radio personalities were the ones who were credited with galvanizing people around the country on this issue, young people were the ones who started that movement. There were e-mails, blogs, and text messages sent all over the country, telling people to get involved and stand up against the injustice handed down to these young men. There were already thousands of people of all ages who were made aware of the situation, because young people were organizing electronically. By the time it reached the national leaders it was already a movement.. These were high school and college students, much like the days of the civil rights movement. Instead of attending mass meetings at churches, they were sending e-mails, informing one another about this issue called the Jena Six.

There are young people on college campuses who are organizing on behalf of janitors seeking a decent and livable wage. There are young people who are standing up against the wars in Iraq and Afghanistan. There are young people on college campuses in Florida who organized against the Juvenile Justice Department over a beating and eventual murder of a young offender. Young people are standing up all over this country; they have the courage to speak truth to power, and they are making no apologies for it. Although their voices aren't heard on radios, and their actions aren't covered on every station, young people continue to organize and speak out against injustice. Although some of their tactics are a little different, they understand the power of numbers, direct action, and the spirit of resistance. There's no question that young people and their courage to act are still alive and well.

The challenge occurs when young activists leave their college campuses or their leaders graduate. They move on to find jobs doing other things. Those who choose to remain in the movement are few and far between. The available options usually offer such small pay with few or no benefits that they choose to do something else with their great talents. Sometimes, the options don't even exist, because the positions are filled with a much older person who is still trying to use 1960 tactics in the twenty-first century.

There's a structural problem within the movement. The critical work that must be done to help move our country in the right direction is often stifled because organizations don't have the capacity to offer the same wages that they fight to get for other people. Some organizations have little or no appreciation for the real experience young people bring to the table, or they are relying on the sometimes antiquated approaches that have proven ineffective.

This doesn't mean that protesting, marching, and other forms of direct action are irrelevant. It simply means that we aren't stuck with an either or proposition. We have to use both approaches, because they can be equally effective if applied appropriately. We send young people the wrong message when we don't make room for their talents within progressive organizations, or when those who support the organizations don't appreciate the need for staffers to make a decent salary to support their families and twenty-first century lifestyle.

There is also a group that is between our generations, which appears to have followed the mold of the elders and old folks. They are elected officials, activists, and genuine "freedom fighters." The problem is, too many of them are broke, or close to it. The end result is that they begin to lose credibility with their work, because they want to get paid for everything they do to help people. The very people they need to help are the ones they try to get paid from.

There was a situation in my own family where my aunt was facing foreclosure. I directed her to one of my colleagues in the legislature. This person had been on television helping families and was supposedly saving their homes from foreclosure and predatory loans. When I sent my family member to this person, he wanted to charge them thousands of dollars to help them save their home. Obviously, if they had that kind of money, they wouldn't have been facing foreclosure. It was shameful at best and pimping at worst. This wasn't the first time that

I experienced such a situation with this one individual. I then joined those who questioned the motives of this person, because he's one way on television but another when the cameras are off. There is a difference between making a decent living from the work that we do and extorting money from people, taking advantage of their desperation because of our own desperation.

I've been in meetings when certain people are disregarded within the community; they aren't trusted or respected because they are broke. They work to help other people, but they can barely help themselves make ends meet. This is what happens when we start out dedicating our lives to good causes but don't prepare ourselves financially. I've always found it fascinating that during the civil rights movement, we had wealthy African Americans who would help to fund the movement; they helped people get out jail, provided legal services, and helped take care of the families of the workers, even though they didn't do much marching themselves. This was their contribution to the movement. Someone had to be there to handle the financial obligations while the movement continued. What we need now is a mixture of that.

For the purposes of wealth-building and wealth-creation in our communities, and for the sake of credibility in our communities, we have to see leaders who are powerful, courageous, and financially stable. This is the model that young people need to see. If we want more young people to carry on this movement, this reality has to be addressed. It's hard for us to do so when we see some of our giants in the community pass away, and then communities have to take up offerings to help support their families. It's a disgrace to their legacy and sends the wrong message to younger generations. We have to shift our paradigm and respect the work of movement workers, both financially and otherwise. Within our institutions, we have to create new structures and implement existing ones that appropriately compensate activists for their sacrifices and work in the community.

We also have to support our organizations that are charged to do civil and human rights work. It's a sad commentary that so many will criticize the work or question the relevancy of an NAACP or SCLC; yet, when someone has a problem at work with discrimination or an issue in the criminal justice system, they immediately pick up the phone to call one or all of these organizations. Some of us get mad at the organizations when we look at who is sponsoring them.

A couple of years ago I refused to attend a luncheon at an NAACP conference because I didn't agree with the business practices of the sponsoring organization. Technically, I have the right to do that. I am a fully paid life member of the NAACP, so I have put my money where my mouth is. Truth be told, I still don't like the practices of this company, but I had to come to understand that the national NAACP has bills, a payroll to meet, and vital work that needs to be done to ensure justice and equality for all people in this country. With that said, the harsh reality is that, although the organization is supposed to depend on paid membership as "the lifeblood" of the organization, it would be extinct if it had to thrive solely on that level of income. Most people are not members of the NAACP.

We should ask ourselves how our organizations are supposed to thrive and focus on the work at hand if we don't support them. How are the colleges and universities supposed to raise additional funds if the people who are the beneficiaries of the education never give back? We have to learn how to support our own organizations so that we won't put them in a position where they are compromised or questioned because of who they accept money from. I am not arguing that, until we get to that place, we should give organizations a free pass to accept money from wherever it comes. There is still a great responsibility on the part of all of our organizations (and individuals) to find the resources to fund their efforts and free themselves of any perception that they are taking hush money or quid pro quo—choosing to ignore a funder's issues in exchange for a high contribution.

While our organizations walk this fine line, we have a tremendous responsibility to support them through our membership and our involvement. We shouldn't get upset when we learn of salaries and benefits for our leaders. Our congress has recently bailed out corporate executives who failed in their jobs; yet we are concerned when the very people who lead our civil rights organizations—sacrificing their time with family and their lives as a whole to fight for the rights of you and me—receive compensation. We have to teach our children the importance of supporting and investing in organizations on the local and national levels. We need to instill in all of us the habit of giving and supporting so that the organizations supporting our causes are strong and without compromise.

I have found myself criticizing elected officials who seem to stay in office forever. For some of them, it's not because they don't want to pass the torch; for some, it's because they have nowhere else to go. Even in my own thoughts about what step could be next for me, I pause, because I think about where I would land if I am not successful. Since I've been elected, I think about having to have five different jobs or contracts. That's because the choices for public servants are so few.

Our organizations and institutions need to create a space for people, those whose hearts are in the right place, to work and earn a decent living so they don't become broke activists or poverty pimps. I think our organizations have to look at how people's skill sets can help further their cause; they need to look at the holistic picture of how our efforts are connected and how the value of supporting courageous elected officials helps sustain the movement. We have to change our mindset and support our own. There are plenty of examples within business and other communities where they take care of their own. We have to do that for one another to sustain the work and sustain who we are as individuals.

We need the courage, energy, and passion of this new generation of leaders who are ready to commit to social change work. We also have to change the paradigm of what activism looks like and how people are able to support themselves. Broke activism simply can't be an option if we are to retain the kind of people we want or sustain the movement we need. We know the need is there. We now have to commit ourselves to supporting the individuals and organizations willing to sacrifice so that we will have the world we each want to live in.

❧ LESSONS I LEARNED ALONG THE WAY ❧

1. Support the organizations that work on our behalf. If we are to help sustain the movement and the efforts of those who are activists, we need to support them financially and with our time. Give back and ensure that our organizations can outlive their purpose.

2. Find ways to become financially stable. Those of us who are chosen to do public service should answer that call with the intent of creating a financial situation that allows us to do the work without compromise. Identify multiple streams of income that allow you to live comfortably while doing the work you are called to do.

3. Teach our children the importance of building wealth and preparing for a rainy day. Perhaps one of the reasons that activists leave organizations or die without the requisite funds is because there was no forethought or preparation for the future. Think now about retirement and the lifestyle you want to live when you are older. Teach our young people about saving, about delayed gratification and preparing for the future. Let's break the cycle of poverty and under-preparedness in our community.

4. Financial stability means freedom and respect. When you have your own money, you don't have to base your lifestyle on the contributions of others. People who have their own money or are financially stable are more respected and relied upon because they are independent. As the saying goes, "Don't send a hungry man home with your lunch." When you are financially stable, you have the freedom you need to make decisions that are in your best interests and that of the community or the people you are attempting to serve.

5. Never become dispensable. Activism is a noble and critical service. Don't choose the issues you work on or the jobs you take based on what you can make. You become the "poverty pimp" when you begin to chase after issues to keep your name out front or the paychecks coming. When the issue runs out or the victory is won, you can become dispensable. Continue to build your craft, develop your skill set, and find ways to keep yourself relevant without compromising your own values.

6. Support your candidates. While we support our organizations and individuals that we like, we also must support political candidates that we like. Both individuals and organizations who expect elected officials to take on their issues should spend their time and their resources to support them. Maybe you can't give thousands, but every dollar and every volunteer hour counts. Organizations can't get involved with campaigns, but individuals who work for them can. Support the people you want to see in office. It takes resources to run campaigns, and those resources should come from supporters, big and small.

11. People over Politics: the Public Servant and the Politician

WHEN I FIRST ENTERED THE legislature, I had no idea what it had in store. It was such a tumultuous time in the state. The new governor had won in an upset election against the incumbent, and the joke was that no one was more surprised than him. In my view, his win was largely because of the low turnout among African Americans, especially in the metropolitan Atlanta area. That low turnout, combined with a historically high turnout among Georgians who wanted to see the return of the Confederate flag in Georgia, made for a victory for Sonny Perdue.

In addition to that, the State Senate was now Republican-controlled, because the new governor had convinced some of the Democrats to switch parties. Then we had a new Speaker of the House after the longest-serving speaker in the history of the country inexplicably lost his seat. Suddenly I was immersed in a time in the state's history that no living person had ever seen. Republicans controlled the governor's office and the State Senate, and we had a new speaker after more than thirty years. This environment was new for everyone.

Although my victory in Cobb County was significant to me, there were lots of other dynamics going on in the legislature that made my first and second term more than I anticipated. It was a new day, and no one really knew how to navigate in those new waters. Not only was I new, everything was pretty much new. Everyone, especially the Democrats, was scrambling, trying to figure out how to navigate these new political circumstances. There was something in the air that caused everyone to fend for themselves and figure out their own way. I did, too.

Because the governor had made a campaign promise to give the "flaggers" a vote on their flag, the issue was at the forefront of my first legislative session. With my background in NAACP, my experience in being an organizer, and coming out of the tradition of speaking truth to those in power, I had no issues standing up against the return of the Confederate flag and saying whatever I felt was necessary in order to make my point. I couldn't believe that in 2003 we were even considering the return of this most hateful symbol of hatred and slavery. But we were, and I felt it was up to me to represent by background, my upbringing, and my life experience as a young black woman. I don't remember my speech, but I can only imagine how inflammatory, loud, yet powerful it was back then.

I remember being disappointed about the vote, and I had a hard time seeing my white colleagues who voted for the Confederate flag as anything other than racists. Something was starting to happen to me and the way I saw my colleagues. The atmosphere in the legislature was so tense. I didn't really know anyone, and no one really knew me. This was my first real introduction to who this black woman from Cobb County was going to be. The bill to put the Confederate flag on a ballot for voters passed the House, but, thank goodness, because of the leadership of then State Senator Kasim Reed and others, the Confederate emblem was removed before Georgians got to vote on our state flag.

The gay marriage fight was much the same. In 2004, President George Bush was running for re-election. He needed an issue that would bring people to the polls, and his camp began the discussions about gay marriage. The Republicans in Georgia felt this would be a great strategy and introduced a constitutional amendment to ban gay marriage. Despite the House of Representatives still being under Democrat control, our then Speaker of the House and other Democratic leadership at the time made the fatal decision that we needed to allow a vote on this most decisive measure. I couldn't have disagreed with them more, and I still hold a great deal of disdain for their misguided decision. I believe that this was the final nail in the coffin that Republicans needed to take control of the third and final leg of the legislative stool, the House.

The gay marriage battle created very similar dynamics to the debate over the Confederate flag. There was so much division between Democrats and Republicans, black and white legislators, and it brought out an even worse sense of anger toward gay people in our state. Much like my response to the debate over the flag, I took to the well and poured out my heart about the need to respect people for who they are and not to write discrimination into the state's constitution. Taking a step further from the Confederate flag, I made some of my points hit close to home.

I remember distinctly pointing out the hypocrisy among members who were so interested in dictating whose bedrooms government should be in and whose it should not. I reminded some of the men how unfair it was that no one was calling attention to their own behaviors that allowed them to have their girlfriends at the capitol and their wives at home. I was stunned by the audacity of many so-called Christians who were so quick to judge an entire group of people who were taxpayers, citizens, and humans—people who were simply different and wanted to live a normal life just like everyone else.

At that time I didn't even have a real position on gay marriage, because no one had ever expressed that as a concern. We already had a law on the books banning gay marriage, and I didn't understand why we needed to include this issue in the document that was designed to give and protect the rights of all people. I now wholeheartedly support gay marriage, because I believe in equal rights for all people, not just the people we think are deserving of those rights or have lifestyles that we are completely familiar with. As a result of that battle, I have become an ally to the Lesbian, Gay, Bisexual, and Transgender community and I am one who believes, as an African American, that the violations of their civil rights are like the violations of the civil rights of black people.

When the constitutional amendment passed the House, I remember feeling angry and hurt at the same time. Between the loss in the House on the gay marriage ban and the affirmative vote for the Confederate flag, I felt myself getting angrier and angrier; I was becoming someone I didn't want to become because of what was happening to me. Not only were we dealing with the most divisive issues possible, but I had a hard time not taking these votes personally. After all, I believed that I was called to serve in the legislature *for a time such as this*. I believed that it was no accident that these issues were coming up at just the right time, because the legislature currently had someone who was willing to speak up in the face of any and all consequences.

In 2005, we had the infamous voter ID issue. This was another issue that cut deep for me because of the work I had done to register people to vote and my commitment to get more people involved in the process. I had taken this issue personally as well. Much like the Confederate flag issue, the black caucus members in both the House and Senate lined up to speak about the injustices of Jim Crow laws and the inability to participate in our democracy because of the color of our skin.

By that third year, I had internalized all those battles over the Confederate flag vote, the gay marriage constitutional amendment, and the voter ID issue. In my mind there was nothing else that could be done to us, and I wasn't sure what could be next. I had so much hatred in my heart. I had no doubt that many of my colleagues had hatred for me. I walked around with a chip on my shoulder, because I found myself in a hell on earth. I was in a situation where I had to be prepared to fight every day, and that became who I was. As much as people in the community appreciated my candor, my heart, and my courage to say what needed to be said, I felt alone and confused about why I had been sent to the legislature. I thought, *surely God wants me to speak truth to those in power, and surely He had prepared me all my life to fight some of the biggest battles I would ever see.* Still, there was something missing. There was something that was happening to me that I just didn't like.

I had a constant inner struggle for months after that. On one hand, I had learned how to define success for myself. My success didn't have to be about the bills I couldn't pass in such a hostile environment. It was about the things I was doing in my district, the minds I could change with my moving speeches and the people who were becoming connected to the process because finally someone was there who was willing to speak up.

Then, I thought, too, about why I wanted to be in the legislature; I had to do some real soul-searching about what I wanted my legacy to be. The powerful speeches, telling it like it is, speaking truth to power, exciting the community, and having no fear were all things I believed were a part of my purpose for being in the legislature. I still believe that. I also started thinking about the opportunity to utilize the environment I was in to make lasting change for the people I represented and for the people in the entire state. While my supporters in and out of the district were completely satisfied with my style of leadership, there was more I needed to define my own success.

I found myself in a constant tug-of-war between wanting to be productive for my district and having to speak truth to power. Some would wonder why there has to be one or the other. It's simple. It's difficult to publicly criticize those who you feel are wrong and then come back and ask them to help you get your bill passed. Until we get more people who are willing to be public servants and others who are willing to stand with them, this is the system.

In the meantime, I find myself trying to walk a thin line. I never want to forsake what I have been called to do in my elected capacity, yet I never want to disappoint those who raised me in the NAACP, other community organizations, and, most importantly, the people I represent who are depending on me to be their voice. I felt like I had to choose between being an activist or a politician.

There were lots of things that happened that year and the next— getting connected to the Young Elected Officials Network, getting more involved in education issues, and even maturing more as a legislator— that helped me hone my leadership style. It's important for me to clarify what I mean by maturing. This is not to be confused with getting older. I have no regrets about my strong stances. The people who were my "mentors" at the time are people who have the same style. They are loud, boisterous, and courageous and have a great deal of support in the community. That leadership style is one that is lauded among certain groups. In fact, during those years, I received many leadership awards and recognitions for standing up for what I believed in. While I appreciate those awards and having the support of many of these same groups, I think we fail to make the necessary progress because we lack any expectation of what should be done besides raising hell.

Despite being younger than the others, I believe I've since matured. I still see them using the same style and still watch how ineffective they are in the process as a whole. My maturation was not about aging but about having a broader picture of what it means to be in the legislature; it was about the great responsibility I have to do more than *just* speak truth to power. It was about personal growth and understanding that becoming angry doesn't change the social ills I was elected and initially ran to try to change.

I went through a metamorphosis and realized that, in order to be effective, I needed to try a different approach. During the first few years of my service, I have no doubt that I served an important purpose. I am now at the point where I want to accomplish more. For those legislators who serve simply to speak truth to power, I say great. This is not a judgment on those who decide to operate in that style of leadership. Everyone has a role to play. I decided that wasn't the role *I* wanted to play any longer.

I wanted to do things differently. I didn't want to become that legislator who turns people off as soon as they start speaking, or the one who looks for fights just to end up in the media. I wanted to make my service mean more. I had to figure out how to find the balance between speaking truth to power and still getting things done. I wanted to find a way to stay true to who I am and the work I've been called to do—and still be effective in the system I was elected to serve.

This was difficult to do. When you are an outsider on the inside, you have to figure out how to navigate those waters. How can you get things accomplished without becoming a part of the very system you are setting out to change? Most people there have learned how to become part of the institution and make it work for them. After all, I had too many examples of what happens when people don't like you or understand you. I didn't want to be the person no one wanted to talk to because I was always angry. Nor did I want to be the person who just goes along to get along. I didn't want to become a "politician". I wanted to be an effective public servant.

Public servants operate from their hearts. They make decisions based on their impact on other people and what they can do to impact the greater good. Politicians operate in a game or war mode. Their decisions are calculated and based solely on getting to the desired result and at any cost. They are willing to wheel and deal and do whatever is necessary to get what they need. I was committed to being a public servant, and I wanted to be able to get things done.

Don't get me wrong, I understand how someone becomes a politician. Politics is a game for most people. If you don't play the game, chances are you will lose. Once you get elected, you learn to play by the rules if you want to be "successful". If you don't, you can be ostracized and marginalized. The people who are quiet and don't make any public challenges are rewarded for their "good behavior" because they aren't seen as troublemakers. They are also rewarded for their silence because they are used to deter "bad" behavior and keep the others in line. I watch my colleagues who want to stand up for what they believe in, but who feel that they can't, because, if they do, they won't get their money in the budget, or the bill they've been working on for three years will never get out of committee. The more they want to avoid the consequences of speaking out, the more they become a part of the institution.

I've also come across individuals who were politicians from the start. They enter the political process because they like the game. If they help people along the way, then so be it. They enjoy the game of power and sitting at the table to decide who gets what—while they take some for their districts as well. This type of politician isn't totally bad, because you need all types in the process who can operate in the current game. Sometimes it takes the politician, who gets to sit in the "room" where decisions are made, to help the public servant—who most likely won't even get to see that room. Everyone has their role to play. You have to find which one works for you. It's a real quandary, and I have learned to try not to judge people who are put in such positions, because we all want to be productive. We all want to go back to our districts and say we've accomplished things. Whether in politics, business, or nonprofits, we all want a role to play and not to just take up space.

A very good friend and preacher, Rev. Markel Hutchins, said to me years ago, "Some of us are tree-shakers, some of us are jelly-makers. You have to decide which one you want to be." I think it's possible to be both, but I agree that you have to decide which one you want to be at particular times. During the civil rights movement, there were many marches and demonstrations that brought public attention to the issues of voting rights and Jim Crow laws. Those who sacrificed themselves by participating in sit-ins, riding on the freedom rides, or providing the money for bail all played important roles. Without the people on the inside—whether they were the negotiators or the members of congress willing to make what could have been considered a courageous vote—we wouldn't have had the Voting Rights Act of 1965. Dr. King had to know when to negotiate and when to protest. Without the role Thurgood Marshall played in arguing the Brown versus the Board of Education case for the NAACP, there would have been no decision from the United States Supreme Court to integrate schools.

We all have our roles to play. The key is being strategic about what role you will play and how everyone else's role fits into what we are trying to accomplish. We need all of the roles to make change. The systems we criticize won't transform by just throwing rocks and expecting things to change. We need the tree shakers on the outside and the jelly makers on the inside—those who are sitting at the table helping to make the decisions, voting for the bill, signing the law, making the decisions for promotions, and arguing on our behalf.

Sometimes I may decide to be the tree-shaker; other times I am the jelly-maker. In the midst of those roles, I've also learned how critical it is to develop strong relationships. I've learned to find issues to work on with people who share common ground. I've seen this as I have worked on education issues. The walls seem to come down when people realize that I'm not angry all of the time, that I'm smart and my heart really is in the right place. They see I am not the angry black woman they perceived me to be, because I try to find issues or a topic that are noncontroversial that we can connect on. I've been more deliberate about smiling, saying hello, and even making jokes to show people a different side of me.

Building one-on-one relationships with people outside of business disarms them. Both sides have an opportunity to see who they are outside of controversy and to get to know one another as people. The first few years, I wasn't able to build relationships because I had to come in fighting. Most of my colleagues never got to see the real me. Now I'm trying to make up for that. I've noticed that the more people get to know the real me the better chance I have to build trust and relationships with my colleagues; the more I am able to successfully navigate the process.

I think the lack of relationships is one of the biggest challenges activists have. No matter what the issue is, if your first interaction with a decision maker is angry or threatening, you don't have a chance to connect or really create an environment for an even exchange. Too often, the first time legislators hear from a group is when they are upset about something. If they would take the time to learn about the legislator and build a relationship, they would be more effective in changing his or her mind or even getting some time to share ideas. In anything we do, relationships help us feel more comfortable with a person. Taking the time to get to know someone for who he or she is might surprise us as we learn that we have more things in common than not. It's easier to get something from a friend than an enemy, or as the saying goes, "You can catch more bees with honey than vinegar." If our organizations are going to make progress, we have to start with building relationships rather than with making demands.

I've made some great strides with my colleagues, especially on the other side of the aisle. While I have no regrets and make no apologies for the strong stances I took, I probably would use different tactics now. It's so important to be more strategic and thoughtful about what you do so that it doesn't get in the way of your overall goals. There's no question that I still have the same stance on the issues. If those issues were to come up for a vote today, I would still vote the same way; I might just approach the debate differently.

Even with my success in passing legislation, I won't cease speaking truth to power. One of the commitments that I have made to myself is to never put myself in a position that compromises who I am. When I feel strongly about something, I won't stand down for the sake of passing a bill or getting some other short-term goal accomplished. When my gut says speak, my soul won't rest until I do; that's how I know which issues I can take on and which I can leave to someone else.

Even when it is difficult and it means sacrificing something that I want, I have to put people and principles over politics. That's what separates those of us who are real leaders. We all have to learn that lesson. My challenges may exist in politics, but this same issue exists in every line of work. You could see injustice at your job, but, because you want the promotion, you are afraid to speak up. You could have a longstanding relationship with someone and refuse to point out his or her wrongdoing, because you are afraid to lose that friendship or you think the person won't like you anymore. That's a real dilemma that we all face at some time or another. I once heard someone use a great analogy. She said, when mom tells you that you were wrong about something, you don't stop loving her because she corrected you. You respect and appreciate the opinion, and you may even correct the behavior.

People respect us when we tell the truth, even if they don't like what we're saying. We have to decide that, rather than becoming like the people we often criticize, we will create a set of ethics where we live by example. The more we play the game or sit idly by in silence for the benefit of self, the more the collective loses out and the less things change. Our job is not to become one of them; it's to foster an environment that creates more of us. Even if the model isn't there, it's up to us to create the new normal, to turn this system upside down and inside out.

❧ LESSONS I LEARNED ALONG THE WAY ❧

1. Never apologize for being true to who you are and what your purpose is. Never get caught up in the game you are trying to play—in politics, at work, at school, or wherever you are—until you become a part of the very system you are trying to change. Listen to your heart. Your heart will tell you when it's okay to let something go and when it's time to speak up.

2. Never underestimate the value of relationships. Having relationships with people helps us to know and understand them outside of conflict. You disagree differently with someone you know and care about. If we start out looking for the best in people, we are more likely to find ways to work through conflict rather than allowing it to escalate. Knowing the people you work with also helps you understand how to communicate with them, and they with you.

3. Create a "kitchen cabinet" or set of advisors to help you navigate your way. Find people you trust, whose opinions you trust, who aren't consumed with your title, and assemble them to advise you. Sometimes, when you are in the midst of things, you cannot see the entire picture. Don't be afraid to ask for advice or consider the perspective of someone who is outside of the process. It's like the sitting-on-the-shoulders perspective. They can see things you can't. The pieces of advice that sit well with your spirit, take; those that do not, leave. Always be open to constructive criticism and willing to change your approach. This only works if you are talking to people you trust and respect.

4. Know your role and when to play it. Whether you are tree-shaker or a jelly-maker, you are needed somewhere in this process. Some of us are needed at the table; some of us are needed on the outside, demonstrating and calling attention to the issues at hand. Everyone has a role; it's up to us to be strategic and to know when and how.

5. Create the new normal. So what if the situation you are in seems too big to tackle and it seems inevitable that we will succumb to the way things have always been? We have been called to create a new normal for ourselves. Whether it's in politics or in life, you don't have to accept the way things are if they aren't helping people. Individuals have changed entire institutions, because they refused to accept the way things are. Normal is what you deem it to be. If you don't like the way things are going, create a new normal.

6. Learn to live for another day. Sometimes we get so caught up in the moment that we forget to see the bigger picture. We can become so emotional that we do and say things we will later regret. Some battles you will win, and some you will lose. Learn which fights are the battles and which are the wars. Nothing is worth losing your dignity and self-respect. If you destroy relationships and tire yourself out on one fight, you can't live (figuratively) to fight the war. Think carefully about what your overall goals are and how you need to get there. Some battles are worth giving up everything for; most are not. Be careful of what you say and how you handle conflict. Your words cannot be taken back. Conduct yourself remembering that you will have to go back to those same people for something else in the future. Learn to live for another day.

7. Don't become what you've set out to change. From the outside, we can criticize the process, a job, or the culture of a place. If we are to learn the rules in order to break them or become an outsider on the inside to create the change that we want, we must be careful not to become the very thing we once despised. If we are to change the systems we despise, we must change the institution without becoming a part of it and repeating those things we want to change.

12. No Permanent Friends or Enemies: Just Permanent Interests

Permanent Friends

I HAVE BEEN VOTING SINCE I turned eighteen. The first time I voted was by absentee when I was a freshman at Clark Atlanta. I don't recall all of the people on the ballot, but I remember I cast my vote for Bill Clinton for president in 1996. If you had asked me then why I voted for Clinton, I probably could not have told you, other than the fact that he is a Democrat. In fact, I would argue that most black people could not tell you why they are Democrats and many Republicans probably couldn't tell you why they vote Republican. They could cite why they are *not* the other, but most people could not give you the affirmative. Why is that?

I cannot speak for Republicans because I am not one. With all of the education I now have about issues, party history, and their ideology, I am pretty sure I wouldn't become a Republican. Both parties benefit heavily from the 50 percent of people in this country who vote strictly down party lines—oftentimes without a thought for who the candidates are, their history, or even their agendas. When it comes to African Americans, we have been voting faithfully for Democrats by at least 95 percent for decades.

It wasn't until I spent a couple of years closely involved in campaigns and the strategies of Democrats that I started questioning why black people would give up so much power and get so little return. For the record, I have just as much frustration about this toward Republicans when it comes to black people. While the Democrats continue to take black votes for granted, Republicans almost entirely ignore black people altogether—with some exceptions.

If you were to consider the hundreds of elections for Democrats that have taken place over the last ten to fifteen years across the country, you would see that black voters have been instrumental in those elections. Even when black voters don't make up the majority of districts or states, their block vote helps to decide elections. Considering the power the black vote has, specifically in electing primarily white Democrats, what have been the overall tangible gains?

Everyone knows the most pressing issues in the black community. We suffer from generations of poverty. In many of our urban areas around the country, public education has become a babysitting service or a prison pipeline; and, in far too many areas, it produces grossly under-educated children. The result is a continued cycle of poverty and lack of opportunity.

Gun violence is the number one killer of black men in this country. The majority of those crimes are being committed by other black men. The penal system is swelling with a disproportionate number of black men. Some of these men wouldn't be there if they had adequate legal representation. The majority of those who fill the prison cells are there for nonviolent crimes, and their prison sentence could have been avoided with drug treatment or employment opportunities.

In no way am I making excuses for the poor choices some black men have made that resulted in prison time, nor am I placing the responsibility for fixing these problems solely on Democrats. I am suggesting that we consider who created the laws and public policy that have helped double and triple the prison population. Who led the charge to incarcerate children in adult prisons? If we did a little research, we'd find that most of the policies were led by white Democrats. I know that's a hard pill to swallow, but I encourage you to check the facts.

In the mid-1990s, I was in high school. I had no idea that I would become an elected official, but I started becoming quite concerned about the laws that were being created that put young people in adult prisons with mandatory sentences. When I got to Spelman, I cross-registered and took a juvenile justice class at Morris Brown. As I learned more and more about the juvenile and adult systems, I discovered a new passion.

Once I got elected to the House of Representatives, I became aware of the laws in Georgia, SB440 and SB441, that prosecutors used to lock up kids as young as thirteen years old for using a bb gun to get two sports tickets. I saw the law used to incarcerate a seventeen-year-old for having consensual sex with one of his classmates. I even visited some of the young people who were incarcerated under these laws and heard the horror stories about being raped inside by older men and not having access to GED classes because they didn't meet the age requirement.

As I researched further, I was appalled to find that the author of these bills that gave a thirteen-year-old a ten-year mandatory sentence in adult prison was not a group of Republicans. It was a group of Democrats. This included the black community's "beloved" President William Jefferson Clinton. You see, President Clinton and then Georgia

Governor Zell Miller were a part of a national movement to "get tough on crime". It was also not by accident that, as states moved in a direction to save us from the "super predator"—the handful of young people around the country who were committing heinous crimes—they needed to pass laws that drew down millions of dollars in federal funding to build new prisons and participate in the war on crime.

Many of these laws were passed under Democratic control. When you mention this to Democrats, there is complete silence, a series of blank faces, or excuses about how they didn't realize the bills went so far. Obviously, we all want to be safe in our communities. I believe that, where there are real criminals, we need to lock up and rehabilitate them so that when they return to our communities they can become productive citizens, not repeat offenders.

When we consider the tragedy we call public education in the urban areas of this country, where there are city school systems like Detroit that are graduating less than 20 percent of their black boys, the Democrats—both black and white—ought to be sounding the alarm and creating policy that will fix the ills that occur in American classrooms each day. Somehow the lack of urgency on our part as African Americans to address these problems ourselves—and the unwillingness to hold accountable both black *and* white elected officials who benefit from our block vote—keeps us in a state of emergency.

Understand my point that when it comes to the black vote, I believe all Democratic elected officials are to be held responsible, myself included. There is just as much blame to go around for those voters who continue to re-elect individuals who don't have to do very much to earn our votes. They still get re-elected because they attend the church chicken dinners, kiss enough babies, or draft enough commending resolutions for the leaders in our community. We continue to elect them without much result because we have such low expectations. Insanity is doing the same thing over and over again and expecting different results. What is it called when you have no expectations at all?

We need to understand the dynamics of power in the political process. If you have votes, you have power, and with that power you make demands. Those demands create the change you wish to see in your communities. When we go to the polls and vote overwhelmingly for any party without asking for or demanding something in return, we allow ourselves to be taken for granted election after election. When we don't use our power, we lose it.

In the Democratic caucus in my legislature, of the seventy-five members that we have, more than forty are black. If the black caucus in the state understood the power we hold in numbers, we would be controlling the agenda of not only the black caucus, but the Democratic Caucus and even the legislature. In my mind, because of the consistent lack of leadership in the black caucus, we have allowed the Democratic caucus to shape our agenda, oftentimes ignoring the issues that need to be addressed in the black community. The same kind of dysfunction seems to exist in many other states in the country.

On the other hand, one group of people in Democratic Party who, despite their small numbers, still wield an incredible amount of power is the Dixie-crats. These are the white, southern Democrats who were Democrats during the Jim Crow era. Historically, we know that it was not the Republicans during Jim Crow who were pushing to maintain segregation. It was the Democrats in the South. Many of the white Democrats in the North switched parties and became Republicans, leaving the southern white Democrats in the minority of a dying breed.

What's ironic is that the vestiges of the southern white Democrats who remain in the party today hold very conservative views, and in Georgia they often vote with the new Republican of the twenty-first century. Some of them have been switching to the Republican Party over the last four to six years. Some, despite their Republican voting record, still call themselves Democrats. Although these Dixie-crats are a real minority in the Democratic caucus in our state, the leadership of the caucus tends to be overly flexible and accommodating toward them, hoping not to risk losing more of them and making the party *more* black. There's something really backward about that thinking. Rather than focusing on the issues that are core to Democratic values, like justice, equality, and opportunity for all people, we cater to the fringe of the party in the name of keeping us all together.

My purpose for pointing this out is not race-baiting. It is to shed light on the lack of real representation and bang for our ballot that black people get for voting over 95 percent for a party that doesn't even respect us enough to address the most serious issues in our community. The truth is, it's not their fault. It's ours. We need to learn the dynamics of power in numbers and the power of accountability. We can't get mad at people who won't create public policy to break cyclical social ills in the black community if we don't have the guts, the unity, or the political savvy to understand the power we give up by letting them do it. Some of the Democratic leaders don't understand these issues because they don't live them. It's up to us to take hold of the power we have and use it to create change.

Permanent Enemies?

The Republicans have given black voters too many reasons not to want to associate, and hence we feel that our only home is the Democratic Party. If they ever want to dismantle the perception that they are racists and exclusionary, perhaps they should consider their stances on issues and stop allowing some of the extreme of the group to set the agenda.

Admittedly, I've never been a Republican. Certainly, from my point of view, this is what it looks like to me.

As a voter, it would be nice to feel like I had a choice in party affiliation. If we are to deal in the reality of American politics, there are really only two choices. Many have pondered the idea of starting an alternate party, or some, like me, have even contemplated becoming an independent. What makes either one of those options less viable is the over 50 percent of people in this country who are married to the parties, whether they even agree with the policy agendas. In the end, those diehard Democrats and Republicans are taken for granted as well, and then the candidates focus on the other 50 percent of Americans who consider themselves independent.

My eight years in the state legislature and watching some of the pressing legislation in the United States Congress prove to me that neither party has a monopoly on great ideas. I believe that the voters, the everyday person who just wants to work hard and enjoy life, could impact this deadlock in the process if we made the parties have to compete to make the quality of life better. Basic bread and butter issues like health care, education, and earning a good wage shouldn't be Democratic or Republican issues; they shouldn't be black or white issues. They should be American issues that are addressed by the people who are elected to serve.

For some, this a new way of thinking. I have colleagues who could never see themselves working with the other party. We've operated for so long in a winner-versus-loser and majority-versus-minority system that putting party aside is a foreign idea. It changes the paradigm of the political power structure that dictates that one party should rule the other. But there is a reason that half of our country refuses to identify with one party or another. These individuals are interested in getting the work done, regardless of the party. The net effect of this old approach is that the people end up losing because politics, egos, and vengeance get in the way of real public policy-making. I do think part of this is a generational thing. As much as Dr. Lowery loves me, he often chides me when he hears about my work with certain Republicans.

I have tried on several occasions to work across the aisle. I have found myself agreeing with Republicans whom I would otherwise be diametrically opposed to on many other issues. The criticisms and questioning that comes from both sides is a travesty. I've seen this happen to others of my colleagues. When they don't walk the line (in either party), the members talk about them behind their backs. They start assuming that you've made some kind of deal, that someone is paying you, or that you must be getting something in return. I know it happens because I used to be part of the group that talked about other legislators when they didn't vote the party line or were seen talking to Republicans. Now I know how it feels.

For too many, it never occurs to them that people have the ability to color outside of the lines, that they were elected to represent their constituents, not the broken party structure. There is certainly a place in this process where party structure and holding the party line according to our values is necessary. Members should take the time to vote based on their own conscience—not fear of losing their chairmanship or office space, being talked about by their colleagues, or losing the support of political groups. There are still lobbyists who don't talk to me today because of one vote on a bill from several years ago. I make no apologies for it, because I was being responsive to my constituents and felt that I was participating in creating policy that would make the system more balanced.

When we become married to the party politics and not to our own values, the legislators aren't the real losers; the people we represent are. The old political adage is, "There are no permanent friends and no permanent enemies, just permanent interests." The interests should be the people we represent and the state and country we want to make a better place to live. Sometimes the Democrats may have a better approach to getting us there; sometimes it may be Republicans. I know too many people who would aggressively disagree with that notion.

I think the new philosophy that we see in President Obama; Deval Patrick, governor of Massachusetts; and many others who are a part of this new generation of political leaders, is that there can be a balance. It is possible to find common ground with people and focus on that rather than the issues that divide us. African Americans in this country need to learn this lesson. Given the current state of the Democratic party and their lack of accountability and results, and the state of the Republican party and its lack of meaningful recruitment, we should find no permanent friends, no permanent enemies—just permanent interests.

Those interests should include creating public policy that will deliver the best public education to all of our children, economic security in our communities, laws in the penal system that guarantee adequate legal representation, and policies that doesn't disproportionally impact any one group of people. That agenda shouldn't be Democrat or Republican; it should just be the agenda of the black community or whatever community. Whichever party can help us achieve it is the one we should work with.

Education has always been my number one issue. It's what is most important to most of my constituents in my district, and it's one of the more pressing issues in states around the country. Along with several other issues, one that I've worked quite a bit on within education is school choice. I strongly believe that parents ought to have the right to choose a school in the public or private sector that best meets the needs of their children. Rather than a child being limited by their zip code, I believe parents should be able to find an education delivery system that gives a child the best opportunity at success possible.

Considering my own educational experiences growing up, I am a product of school choice. I attended a majority white elementary school in Miami because my mother chose to take advantage of a minority to majority school program (also known as the M to M transfer program). My mother chose Highland Oaks Elementary School because she thought it was a better educational opportunity; she wanted me to be around a more diverse group of students, and the school was close to my father's job, so he could take me back and forth to school when necessary.

From there she continued to exercise choice as I attended the magnet middle school for theater, then a performing arts school for high school. Attending those schools of choice have shaped who I am today. The choices my parents made for me opened a world to me that many kids are never exposed to. Those life experiences made me a more well-rounded child and helped me to understand the world beyond the walls of my home or the boundaries of my neighborhood. If it were not for the choices my parents had access to, I would have had no exposure to faiths or cultures different from my own; to hundreds of plays and their different genres; to the eighth grade trip to New York (where I met Malcolm Jamaal Warner), or even to the national theater award I received for my abilities in acting. Too many parents in this country don't have choices, and their kids are stuck in schools that aren't meeting their needs. I want kids to have opportunities similar to the ones I had.

My own experiences strengthened my resolve to use my position as a state legislator to help create those opportunities for young people today and for generations to come. The sum of those life experiences have helped shape my views on what public education should look like and the need to open those opportunities for all children. Somehow those life experiences have pitted me against the people in my own party. Each time we have considered education policy that is different from the traditional delivery system of public education—no matter how broken, tattered, or a proven failure the current system is for far too many children—the resistance often comes from primarily Democrats as well as Republicans who work in that system.

In no way am I suggesting that all traditional public education is broken. What I am suggesting is that in the twenty-first century, educating our children the same way we were educated in the twentieth century seems regressive at best. I find that many of my colleagues are simply more comfortable with the way things have been for fifty years or more and intend to continue in that vein. They romanticize how wonderful things were when they were in school, and they believe that's how education still is.

Ironically, I find that most of these defenders of status quo fall into one of three categories: they have adult children who have long exited the public education system; they have children who have never seen the inside of a public school because they only attended private schools; or they don't yet have children, so it is easy to make policies that have no direct impact on their families. They don't know what it's like not to have real choices in the most important decision a family can make for their children.

This is the first time in my political life that I find myself in a real quandary. The people I consider to be political friends don't understand my views, my life experience, or how I have arrived in this place of working with the "enemy"—in this case, Republicans. There are a few things to put out for the purpose of full disclosure. First, I too used to be one of those Democrats who didn't trust anything a Republican said. In fact, if I found myself on the same side as a Republican on a particular issue, I would have to think twice because that meant I must have been wrong. Second, I am keenly aware of the segments of the education reform movement whose ideology and motivation for school reform is steeped in re-segregation, under-funding public education, and wanting to privatize every public entity because they don't like government. I generally think these ideas are radical, out of the mainstream, and pitiful. I also think that this segment is small and insignificant when you consider that public education in most states is a constitutional right (and should be in the United States Constitution—but I digress).

Third, I will make it known that my husband, who has over fifteen years of experience in education as a teacher and principal (the bulk of those before we even met), is presently a lobbyist for a school choice organization and also serves on the local school board in our district. I point these out up front so there won't be a focus on his work rather than on the merits of this issue. Hopefully, my own life experience and commitment to empowering others provides the background for understanding how I've come to my conclusions on choice and other issues in education reform.

Sadly, many of my Democratic colleagues cannot move past my husband's work in this area. They find themselves stuck on his current affiliations and can't seem to grasp the thought that I have the ability to think for myself or that I have my own history. They disregard the fact that my eight years on the education committee and my twelve years of primary and secondary educational experience spans beyond my time of even knowing David. Despite my record of being independent and strong-willed, that history gets ignored. I think the juicier story is that David and I are conspiring and taking over Georgia with our plans to implement vouchers and destroy public education.

These aren't things I've made up. These are things I have actually heard people say or write in e-mails to me. They believe that my husband is influencing me and somehow we both benefit financially from my stances on education issues. They refuse to consider my real and unapologetic commitment to reforming public education. This presents quite a frustrating struggle for me. It does so because I find myself isolated from the people who have always been my allies and connected to the people I have always distrusted because their motives *seemed* unscrupulous and seemed to exclude entire groups of people.

This is why you have to be clear about your purpose. I believe it's not by accident that this issue has become the most passionate one for me, despite the political and personal obstacles it creates for me. It's my test of real leadership to be able to stand firm on what I believe, despite how unpopular it is among my colleagues and among the status quo.

Working on this issue has also been a blessing in disguise. One of the reasons David is so happy in his life is because of his passion for education and the work he is now doing to reform it. He spent years in the classroom trying to help students and provide opportunities for them, despite what was going on at home. He's fired up when he gets up in the morning, because his life's work has meaning. As challenging as it is to hear the rumors and experience the backbiting—and no matter how much easier my political life would be if one of us chose another issue—for me family comes first. Education is the issue that has chosen us both. The last thing I would do is stand in the way of my husband's purpose because of what's easier for me politically. Nor would I forsake what I've been called to do because something has become too hard.

I've accepted that I will always have a question mark by my name when it comes to my education work, because people don't always know the whole story or even attempt to learn it. But as long as I can be a part of the new civil rights movement to reform education, that's a burden I'm willing to carry. Besides, David and I working on this issue together (even in those times when we may disagree) brings us closer together and causes us to spend more time together. Who wouldn't want to work with their best friend? This issue gives us both something to work towards, something to work to achieve that's bigger than us.

During the 2008 session, I found myself working with a prominent Republican from the state Senate. He had a checkered legislative history on some of the most divisive issues we've faced. Those were challenging enough circumstances, but to make things worse, the work I was doing with him was on a voucher bill. Oh, no, I said the v-word. For the most politically involved individuals in America who consider themselves Democrat, you can differ on many issues; but the ultimate litmus test is where you stand on vouchers.

Through my upbringing in the NAACP and my involvement in politics, I was very much indoctrinated that Democrats and progressives hate vouchers, and *we* do everything in our power to stop them. I felt that way and held up the anti-voucher banner like a true Democrat should—until I started talking to everyday parents who aren't caught in the political games. I started understanding the importance of creating opportunities for real school choice, primarily in the public sector, and then in the private sector as well. I started understanding that affluent families (including many of my colleagues) have always exercised the ultimate school choice by either sending their children to private school or moving into the areas with the best public schools.

I can't be mad at them. David and I will do the same thing with Lailah. I realized what I needed to do is work to create opportunities so that all children, regardless of their socioeconomic status, have access to as many opportunities as possible. I stop short of saying creating all of the opportunities that the affluent have, because I understand that some schools, some opportunities, are simply not financially possible. While I can't provide every opportunity, I can do my best to provide as many as possible.

I had a school in my district that, at the time, had never in its history made Adequate Yearly Progress (which is a federal standard set in the No Child Left Behind Federal Education Law). I kept hearing the frustration and hopelessness in the voices of parents in my district who felt they had no real choices to educate their middle school child. As a policy maker, a parent and a person who cares deeply about empowering people, how much longer was I going to look them in the eye and say, "I'm sorry, this is your only option"?

A voucher was not going to be the solution to the problems that existed in the school at the time, nor was a voucher going to provide the real school choice parents deserved. But at the time, this voucher bill could have been a short-term fix and one of the options for these parents who needed help—not when we finally prioritized fixing the problems in that school, but right then when they needed the relief and a shot at a quality education. For the first time in my life, I found myself opening my mind to something I had been taught to hate for as long as I can remember.

As I wrestled with what I thought was right for students in a dire educational situation, I weighed the consequences of that decision. I thought about how my colleagues would abandon me and talk about me behind my back. I thought about the allegations that would be made that I was selling out or getting something in return. I thought about the teacher's union that supported me and how that one vote could erase my 100 percent voting record on their issues over the last six years.

I thought long and hard about all of the consequences that would come along with that vote. I knew at the end of the day, if I was going to vote for the bill, it would have nothing to do with any of those factors or even what I could get in return. I knew it would have to be about those children, who weren't Democrat or Republican, who weren't the first priority for the teacher's union, but needed to be my first priority. I decided I was going to vote for the bill.

In my desire to prepare for what would be one of the most important votes that I would make in my legislative career, I continued to wrestle with what I would say. I looked at the research and saw the number of failing schools across my state, the majority of them with black and brown students in them. I thought about the entire education system. I pulled together a little kitchen cabinet meeting, and I listened to the people I trusted mull over what I should say. We created a speech called, "Time to trouble the waters."

The day we were to vote on the bill, I felt heavy in my heart the entire day. I knew that many people wouldn't understand my decision, but it was something I had to do. I knew there would be grave consequences, but I was willing to accept them because that's what leadership is.

I never got to give that speech because the bill got caught in political wrangling the last day of the session. I realize now that the experience was not really about the speech that I was to give. It wasn't only about the issue of education. It was about testing my own values and the commitment I've made to ensuring that every child has an opportunity to receive a quality education. This moment forced me to consider what I thought about the issue and how my actions lined up with my words, as opposed to what the union and the NAACP told me to think. I began then learning the hard way that there is no such thing as permanent friends or permanent enemies, just my permanent interests. I had the misfortune of having to learn that firsthand as the session ended, but the grief caused by my intention to vote for a voucher bill didn't end with the session.

Since 2008 was an election year, I was up for re-election. I had not started raising money yet, but one day I opened the mailbox and, to my surprise, there were two checks for $2,300 each. That was the maximum amount a person or company could contribute to a campaign. The checks were from the senator I was working with on the voucher bill. It was another moment when I would have to figure out what to do.

These were two contributions, one for my primary election and one for my general election, that I hadn't requested and I certainly didn't know were coming. I knew that if I deposited the checks, it would stoke the fire on the Democratic side that I was being paid off for my vote or that this was somehow connected to my husband's line of work. I knew that all kinds of rumors would start the minute people found out about this contribution. I also knew that, because I didn't solicit these campaign contributions, they were sent with no expectations. I did later find out that there were at least two other Democrats he had sent campaign contributions to, and mine was sent because of my willingness to be courageous.

This was another important decision for me, because I knew that this would deepen the wounds being created by my openness to the voucher discussion. Just as I expected, the rumors started. I read about the contributions on a couple of blogs, and it was even written about in a few local newspapers. Although many had their assumptions, not one person picked up the phone or sent me an e-mail to ask me where I stood on the issue, what was factual, what wasn't, or even if there was a connection to the contributions my campaign received. Rather than call someone to find out the truth, sometimes it's easier for people to create their own. And they did.

Shortly after that, several political action committees (PACs) started meeting about candidate endorsements for the elections. On at least three occasions, I heard that part of the considerations regarding whether the PACs would support me, were discussions about the work my husband does, the contributions I received, and the "almost" vote I cast for vouchers. Two of those organizations' "special interests" had nothing to do with education. It didn't matter though. Typically, when making decisions about endorsing candidates, women's choice groups don't care if you are against the death penalty, and education organizations don't care about your position on stem cell research; but for some reason, when it comes to vouchers, it's the one nonnegotiable for Democrats.

These two groups actually had individuals in their meetings who pushed for not supporting me because of a vote that hadn't even happened. Even if the vote had happened, do I not have the right to think for myself? Shouldn't I have the opportunity to look at each issue individually? It was pretty amazing. I did end up getting the support of all of those groups, with the exception of the state teacher's union. Despite my 100 percent voting record over six years, based on one vote that might have happened, I lost their support. I knew that my decision to support the voucher bill would have its consequences, and I have accepted that as one of them. The senator who sent me that contribution had his own problems on his side of the aisle to deal with as well. Just as the attacks continue on my side, he too endures his share of it, neither of us apologizing for finding unlikely allies on this important issue.

The 2009 legislative session continued to teach me to have no permanent friends and no permanent enemies, and it rang true then, more than ever before. I didn't know the real meaning of permanent issues until I introduced HB 251. Without going into a policy discussion here, I'll just say that I wanted to provide students the opportunity to transfer to schools within their public school district. Many states already had this kind of policy. I wanted to extend this to our students. It's my belief that parents ought to be empowered to make decisions that are in the best interest of their children and families, rather than the school district.

When this bill first came to the House floor, there was a great deal of support for it. Ironically, I presented the bill on the day I was hosting my Annual District Lobby Day at the Capitol for my constituents. This is my signature event where I bring at least one hundred students and constituents to the capitol to spend the day and get a firsthand experience of the legislative process. This day they saw more than I could have planned.

The only major opposition, sadly from one of my colleagues from my own home county, this legislator opposed the thought of *those failing kids coming from those failing schools to the schools in his district.* I'm not sure what was worse, the fact that he believed that the kids and the schools were all failing or the fact that he said such ignorant things in the presence of those so-called "underperforming kids" he was referring to. Despite his ignorance, the bill passed 129 to 34. A little secret is that I didn't cast my vote for my own bill that day; I was so busy watching the board for everyone else's vote.

Once the bill left the House and went over to the Senate for its vote, some drastic changes were made. I had made the commitment that 251 was not going to become a vehicle for vouchers (limited scholarships given to public school students to attend a public or private school of their choosing). Other changes, I would not be able to control.

Once a bill goes from one house to another, the author of the bill has very little control over what another chamber does to amend the bill in any way. The author always has the ability to keep the bill from moving, but just getting a bill through the process—from introduction, through the committee process, through the Rules committee (which is the gatekeeper committee that determines if a bill will get to the House or Senate floor for a vote), onto the floor with the requisite number of votes, and on to the next chamber—is hard enough.

To stop it once it gets to the next chamber is an exercise in futility. If you've gone through all of that process in one chamber, you tend to want to do whatever it takes to get it through that same process in the other chamber so it can go on to the governor for a signature. In no way does that mean that I would allow just anything to be added or taken away from the bill, but it means that we are all more likely to compromise so that, at the end of the process, we still create the public policy we intended.

When HB251 got to the Senate, it became a very attractive vehicle for other bills that had not passed, meaning that other bills could be attached to mine. It's a common practice in the legislative process. Legislators are so eager to get their bills passed that attaching theirs to something that appears to be moving still gives them an opportunity to get it done, even if they are no longer the primary author. In many discussions with a few of the leaders on the Senate Education committee, it was very clear to me that the version that passed the House would become very different.

The Senate Education committee added another bill onto HB251 that would not only allow students to transfer within their own school district, but would also allow transfers outside the district. I wasn't opposed to the change, as I support all school choice, especially within the public sector. I also knew that many districts in the state had only one school at each level, so transferring within the district would not have been a real option for those students. I knew it would be a challenge to pass this new version, but I knew it would be important to maintain the support of the senators who would vote for the bill. In no way was I compromising beyond my own beliefs. If I hadn't believed in the changes, I would have fought against the change or just withdrawn the bill. I had already been in hours of negotiation with some powerful senators to get the version that we ended up with. There were some points that were critical for me and others that I compromised on so that we could move the legislation forward.

A firestorm started. While many parents appreciated the idea of being able to send their child across district lines, the status quo education experts (i.e., many school board members, school superintendents, the teacher's union, and many other groups entrenched in the century-old education system) launched strong opposition to the new version. I found myself standing before the Senate Democratic caucus the day of the vote on HB251 feeling like I was in a room of opponents. Questions were fired back and forth. I defended my new bill to the best of my ability, but the status quo had already gotten to them, and nothing I said could convince them that this was not a ploy to destroy Georgia's public schools or bankrupt poor districts by allowing students to leave for better options.

One legislator even told me that her district had lost enough money, so she could not support this bill. Students leaving the district means losing money, because the dollars assigned to each student follow them to the school of their choice (as I believe it should be). It seemed that the discussion was never about what was best for the child or the family. The debate had never risen to be about the merits of school choice, instead the background discussions were about my integrity and motive for working on this legislation.

After I presented and responded to every question presented to me, I was made to leave the room (despite being a fellow colleague) so that the teacher's union and the other status quo organizations could enter to make their case. I had never been asked to leave a meeting of legislators. I felt disrespected and disregarded, even mistrusted. Despite my individual calls to almost every member of the Senate Democratic Caucus—some of them making affirmative commitments, others saying they would support it as long as it did not become a voucher bill—only one Democrat in the caucus voted for the bill in the end.

In fact, that one vote was the decider as the bill passed the Senate in its new version with the smallest majority required. There are fifty-six senators, and the bill passed with twenty-nine votes. In fairness, there were plenty of other issues, personality conflicts, and a history of mistrust with the Republicans who had now become champions of the bill on the Senate side. All of those things took center stage over the merits of the bill. Nevertheless, as we all know, every vote counts. Whether you win by five thousand votes or one vote, a win is a win.

The rumor mill grew larger and the backbiting grew stronger. I was surprised by the Senate Democratic caucus response; I was flabbergasted by the House Democratic response. Because the original version of HB251 had changed, the bill would have to go back to the House for our chamber to agree or disagree with the changes that were made by the Senate. Before the bill even got back to the House, the Senate members and education status quo who were the ringleaders of the voucher circus had already had conversations and warned the House Democratic leadership and any other members who would listen. One of the teachers' groups that had supported the original bill was now working overtime to oppose it, sending out statewide alerts, and setting up meetings with the House Democratic Leadership.

The House Democratic Caucus held a policy meeting to discuss pending legislation and HB251 came up. It was already abnormal for a bill introduced by a Democrat to even be discussed. Because the number of Democrats in the House who pass bills is so small, the discussion is normally around Republican-sponsored bills. Not only was my bill brought up, but side discussions ensued about my campaign contributions, why I would even introduce this legislation, and who was really behind it. It was as if many of these people hadn't been serving with me all this time, as if they didn't have a record to call upon for me. Some of these comments were made were from people I thought were friends.

It was decided that the caucus would not take an "official" position against the bill. Instead, they would encourage all members to vote against it. I'm not sure what the real difference is, and no one to this day can explain it in a way that makes any sense to me at all. Despite the lack of support from my own caucus, I had to get over it. I continued to secure votes from both Republicans and Democrats, legislators I knew supported public school choice, some of whom were willing to buck the leadership and do what they thought was right. The next day in the full caucus meeting, I made sure I was there. Oftentimes I would miss caucus meetings because so many of us are frustrated with what appears to be a lack of real leadership within the caucus. But that's another topic for another book.

During the caucus meeting, I listened to debate go back and forth about numerous bills. The caucus took positions on some bills; on others, where the leadership was clearly divided, we voted not to take a position at all. When my bill came up, I asked for the opportunity to speak. I urged the members of my caucus to vote in favor of the bill and explained the merits of the bill. I also urged them to take the personal attacks out of it and vote based on the merits, not on anything else.

I was fed up with all the talking behind my back while smiling to my face. I know it happened more than I was made aware of because I used to be one of those people. If I had seen that someone was getting a bill passed or getting money in the budget for their district, I would assume that they must have made a deal or sold their soul because, after all, Democrats couldn't get any bills passed. At least, that's what I and so many of us had convinced ourselves to believe. For some Democrats who tried to pass bills, it was very true. For other Democrats, failure to pass a bill was not because the Republicans hated them or were unwilling to let their bills move, but because those Democrats hadn't introduced any bills in the first place.

It was the mindset of defeatism. If you start out saying what you can't do and what's not going to happen, you are exactly right. Eventually it becomes a self-fulfilling prophecy. Not every bill I introduce will be passed, and there will be sessions where I can't get any passed. It's not always because I am in the minority party. Sometimes it's because my colleagues don't agree with the public policy I am trying to create. Sometimes it's just politics. There are Republican legislators with bills that will probably (and hopefully never) pass.

But, because I have been there, focusing on all of the negative, I have been one of those people making personal attacks on people whose circumstances I didn't even know. Because I'd been present when legislators talked about another legislator—either contributing to the talk or remaining silent—I was all too familiar with what I was now taking the brunt of. Everyone has his own approach. Mine was to deal with this head-on and give notice to those colleagues I thought were friends that I knew what was going on; more importantly, I reminded my colleagues about the need to have substantive conversation over policy and especially education reform.

In my seven, now eight, years there, I had never seen our caucus discuss real education reform. We were always prepared to fight the governor on what he was trying to do, and in some cases we supported his efforts. For the most part, we never had any policy discussions or debates on anything other than the small impact policies like class size and education funding cuts. This whole HB251 battle was a great example of that. I knew that the issue had very little to do with me; it was more about the personalities involved and their hostility toward any change in the system. At that particular caucus meeting, we did have some discussion around HB251 and the transfers within public schools.

During that meeting there was a commitment to have more discussions, and I am still looking forward to that happening.

Despite working to secure votes in favor of the new version, including a close friend who was a little afraid but committed to stick with me, we were unsuccessful, and the Senate language was stripped from the bill. Although some new language had remained, the original intent of the bill allowing transfers only within the school district was passed out of the House. I had no problem with that because, after all, as long as my original bill passed, we would still be able to provide many students with the opportunity to transfer to schools within their districts.

The story doesn't end there. The bill then had to go back to the Senate for them to *insist* or *recede* from their position. This means that I had to go back to the Senate and shore up the votes for the original bill. I knew that there were some who didn't think the original bill did enough and others who had supported the original bill but were now upset because of all of the wrangling around it. This was now the last week of session, and I only had a few days to make this work. I was looking at every parliamentary procedure, every possibility that could play out to make sure I was prepared for whatever could happen. My bill was now in the posture of the Senate having to vote on it again; it could come back to the House for a response to whatever the Senate said; and I had to know all of the possible procedures beyond that—all with one day left in session.

The Senate Republican leadership had decided that they could still support the original version of the bill, but I still was not home free. The last two to three days of our legislative session are the craziest, because every legislator with a bill that isn't moving and falls in the same code section as your bill— which *is* moving—wants to make your bill a vehicle to add their bill to. My bill was held for several hours, along with many others, while other negotiations and games took place. The

House leaders wanted their bills passed and would, in turn, hold up Senate bills. It's one of those horse-trading games that drive me crazy, because everyone has something that's important to them that will help as many people as the next bill and this is their last chance that year to move it forward.

My bill was treated no differently. I continued to work on the votes in both chambers to prepare for the bill moving at any time. At first I was told my bill would move with no additional amendments. That was good news, as I had already been talking to the governor's staff to make sure the governor didn't have any issues with it. Any changes would kick-start conversations all over again. I continued to wait that day and into the evening before I would hear anything. The Senate leaders then decided to keep the bill in play, choosing to insist on their position. The bill came back to the House, where I had to ask the house to insist on our position and have a conference committee appointed.

A conference committee has three members of the House and three members from the Senate. To take it to a vote in both chambers you need four of those six to sign the report signifying they agree with the report. Once the Speaker appointed the committee that included me as the author of the bill, we went to work. I got legislative counsel to draft the bill that we needed with all of the key people's concerns included and had it printed. Since it was back to the original version, the two House members signed. When I got over to the Senate, I expected the same speed but was met with yet another bump in the road.

Around 9:00 pm on the last day of session, one of the Senate leaders came over to me and strongly suggested that I add to my bill another bill that had been lost in the process. This was an issue important to another Senate leader, and, because one of the governor's bills that included this issue had not passed, it needed to be added to mine. Now I had two choices. With just three hours left in session for the year, I could say yes and risk another fight with legislators who I knew had problems with that part of the bill. Or I could say no and risk the bill dying all together. This is one of those moments where you must weigh your choices: fight to the end and know you've done your best, or say, "I've done all I can do and I will try again next year."

I thought about the e-mails I was getting from parents who wanted to access HB251. I thought about all of my mom's co-workers who were sending e-mails and making calls. I thought about all of the work my legislative aide and interns had done to move HB251 forward. I thought about how we had come so far and about how irritated I was that, although I had been told hours earlier that the bill wouldn't be amended, things had changed anyway. I thought about what it would take to have to start all over again next session.

Most importantly, I thought about the thousands of young people who would be stuck in a school that didn't meet their needs for another year. I thought about how crucial it is to act with a sense of urgency when it comes to education reform. After a few more conversations with key people in the Senate, I realized that if I wanted any chance of moving this bill this session, I needed to add on that second part. So I did.

We went back to legislative counsel and got another conference committee report drafted that included the new language. Time was of the essence. We were up against the clock. Every signed conference committee report had to sit on the desk at least one hour before it could be voted on. That meant that we needed our bill to be on the desks in the House and the Senate by 10:59, since the session ended at midnight on the fortieth day. We rushed to get the new language in, have the bill written and go through the legal process, get it signed by at least four members of the six-person committee, and then printed and out on the desks.

Finally, we got all of that done close to 10:00 pm. We went back to the original bill allowing transfers within the district and added the new part for the Senator. The vote came up in the House first. I went to the well to present the bill. It would have been easy for me to not even mention the new part that had been added to the bill. There were numerous other bills that were facing the same time constraints, and this was the time during session when crazy things could happen, because most legislators were busy watching for their own bills or paying attention to ensure nothing crazy got slipped in and passed because of haste.

My own integrity dictated that, despite the opposition to the new part of the bill, I needed to be open and honest about what was in the bill. I did. I explained the new part, answered questions, and asked my colleagues to vote for the conference committee report. I took my seat and the bell started ringing. That's the signal to legislators that it was time to vote. The speaker ordered the voting machines opened and members of the house cast their votes. It was 11:22 pm.

Despite needing at least ninety-one to pass any legislation, the bill failed seventy-seven to seventy-eight. I was shocked, upset, and everything else you could imagine. I immediately asked for reconsideration so that I could shore up more votes and then have us vote on the bill again. I didn't know where the votes would come from, but I was not going to give up.

Then something crazy happened. The man who just four years prior had been my nemesis became my saving grace that night. The Speaker knew how hard I had been working on that legislation. He ordered all members of the House to come back into the chamber and the doorkeepers to lock the doors. There are 180 members of the House, and only 155 members had voted. Some were either "walking" on the vote or they weren't in the chamber. He reminded the members that when the bill came through the first time it had passed overwhelmingly. When you see the Speaker go to such lengths, he is typically sending a signal to his party that this is something that he wants and is encouraging their support. Ultimately, every legislator has to make his or her own decision, but it helps a great deal when the Speaker is locking the doors and requiring every member present to cast a vote.

He ordered the machines open and had the clerk ring the bell. "All members voted" he called. "The clerk can lock the machine." This time, at 11:24, the vote was 103 to 62 for the House to reconsider its action. This didn't mean the bill had passed, this just meant the bill was reconsidered and we would vote on it again. I zipped out of the House chamber over to the Senate to let them know what was going on. My goal was to get them to help me get the votes we needed to get to ninety-one. They were involved with all the other bills they had going and no one could really help. I dashed back over to the House and started working the floor. I had until 11:59, and I was going to work until the last second. I spoke to Republicans and Democrats. I spoke to white and black legislators, rural and urban. I went to every person I could to see if I could explain any issues they might have had, to talk about the impact of the bill, or to simply beg.

Time was running out, and it was time to go back to the well and make my plea one more time with my colleagues in the House. I went to the well and simply said, "With every bit of humility in me, I ask the members of this House to vote to adopt the conference committee report for HB251." There was nothing else I could say or do or explain. This was it. As I walked back to my seat and listened to the bell ring, I prayed. I asked God to do what only He could do because I had done all I could do. At 11:47, the speaker ordered the machines locked, and the vote was ninety-seven to seventy-three. It had passed the House!

One huge hurdle was crossed, but there was one more to go. Now we needed the Senate to adopt the report as well. With just twelve minutes left, I ran to the Senate chamber as fast as I could to let the leadership know that the bill had finally passed the House and I needed it to pass the Senate. As the message got up to the lieutenant governor who presides over the Senate (like the Speaker does in the House), he called HB251 up for the vote. There was so much mayhem going on as the clock ticked away. All I wanted were those twenty-nine votes. At 11:53 pm, the Senate voted forty-two to eleven, adopting the conference committee report, thus passing HB251. Whew! With a whopping seven minutes 'til midnight, we had done it.

We still had to endure the waiting process for the governor to sign the bill. Many legislators had gone through similar experiences only to have the governor veto the bill, so we knew we still had more work to do. There were many efforts on the part of school board groups and other bureaucrats within the education system who tried to convince the governor to veto the bill. We certainly did our due diligence on our part to get parents and other advocates to ask the governor to sign the bill.

Finally, on May 5, 2009, my second bill was signed into law. With so many lessons in that experience and the tremendous preparation for what I know is yet to come, the most critical lesson I learned was that we have no permanent friends and no permanent enemies.

No one could have convinced me even two years earlier that the very people I counted as friends—friends who attended my wedding and threw me a baby shower—would be some of the same people standing in the way of my bill, questioning my integrity, or talking behind my back. No one could have convinced me that the people who once talked about expelling me from the legislature—people who wanted a public apology for standing up for what I believed in, people who orchestrated the Voter ID bill—would be the same people who would help me move one of the most important pieces of legislation I would pass in my legislative career.

This experience tested much of what I believed about entire groups of people on both sides. It opened my eyes to my own errors. It made me think about those times I questioned another legislator's integrity, how I would participate in conversations criticizing Republicans as a whole or Democrats who were passing bills. Being on the other side of that criticism made me change how I see other people and, more importantly, how I see myself. The process of getting HB251 passed helped me to learn the difference between my colleagues and my friends. No matter what the issue is, real friends don't question your integrity. Friends don't participate in conversations about you in your absence and contribute to the backbiting. Friends will disagree with you on an issue but they don't allow it to get personal. Colleagues are people who work with you but have no real personal connection. They aren't bound by the code of friendship that ensures they have your back at all times.

I learned these things the hard way, but it's a lesson I won't have to learn again. I'm different, and I see my colleagues differently. Never in a million years would I have thought that Earl Ehrhart would become my partner in education reform when I was a student marching against his bill in 1999. Who would've thought that the speaker would help save *my* bill in the last minutes of a legislative session? Who would've thought that one of my sorority sisters would lead the charge to kill my bill in the House? Well, it happened. Because of it, I have now made it my policy in politics to have no permanent friends or permanent enemies, just permanent interests.

Next session it could be back to the Republicans pushing some crazy effort and the Democrats having to band together to stop it. I've seen both sides, and I understand that I will focus on issues, not who I think my friends or enemies are. I will think about what's in the best interest of the people I've been elected to represent. Unfortunately, the challenges continue now that I am focused on the area of teacher effectiveness. Whatever the issue, I try to figure out who I might be able to work with to achieve the best education system for every child in my state. In fact, because of my work and willingness to speak truth to power when it comes to education, I've been asked to travel to different states to speak to fellow legislators and parents about the need for reform.

From a broader perspective, I have also come to realize that this may not be the only issue where Democrats could be totally off base. It's a lesson for me that it's important to think for myself and understand why I have positions on issues rather than following the party line or reciting the talking points. My constituents deserve more. They elected me to represent their values and to work toward policies that will better their lives. From this point on, I am grounded in who I am, what my purpose is, and what my permanent interests are. I no longer have permanent friends or permanent enemies, just the permanent desire to create change, challenge the status quo—regardless of their party affiliation—and make no apologies for it.

Working with unlikely allies is not just a political phenomenon. There are people in workplaces who are trying to get the work done, not make friends. Sometimes we don't always like the people we are paired to work with or even the people who become our bosses. We have to take personalities out of it and figure out how to get the job done. With one goal in mind, you can take the focus off who your friends are, who are supposed to be your enemies, and focus on the permanent interests—which should be to do well in achieving the goal placed in front of you. Anything else is focusing on the wrong thing.

❖ LESSONS I LEARNED ALONG THE WAY ❖

1. Never apologize for making the distinction between your colleagues and your friends. If you make the distinction early on, you can manage your expectations for both. Don't assume that people are your friends because they are friendly with you or have some things in common with you. It's okay to separate your professional and personal lives. Allow yourself the space to keep work stuff at work and personal things to yourself.

2. Keep your eyes on the prize. Never get bogged down in what people say, what they think your intentions are, or how they feel about what you are doing. When you are a person of integrity, your record will supersede rumors, haters, and those who don't have goals of their own. Stay focused on the goal in mind. There will be distractions along the way, but try not to expend your energy on them. Keep your eyes on the prize.

3. Keep looking in the mirror. Sometimes when we are at war, whether in politics, at work, or wherever it may be, it's human nature to be affected by what people say and think about you. You should get up every day and keep looking in the mirror. If you like the person you see and are proud of the decisions you have made, keep doing what you are doing. If you can continue to look yourself in the mirror and there is honor and dignity in the person who is looking back at you, remind yourself that you are doing the right thing.

4. Stop and ask yourself how this is working for you. Always take time to review the goals that you have set for yourself. When you are in the midst of the process, stop and ask yourself if the approach you are using—and sometimes the hell you are going through—are helping you get to your final goal. Ask yourself how this approach is working for you. If it's not, stop, refine, and try a different approach.

5. Watch how you treat people along the way. Sometimes in the midst of a crisis we say things we later regret. Always remember that if you are to live for another day, maybe you should go for a walk instead of telling that person off. You may have to work with that person in the future and you'll be glad you reserved all of the cursing for your empty office or the friend who let you vent. Avoid ruining relationships. Think carefully about the long-term effects of your actions and your words.

6. Never make permanent decisions in temporary situations. My pastor often says this, and I think it's one of the most powerful things I've ever heard. Whether it's your words, getting back at someone, or deciding who you sleep with, make decisions based on your long-term plans, not on that current situation. So many situations pass and relationships go away. When you make permanent decisions in a temporary situation, you end up facing the consequences long after that situation is over. Think carefully about how you react to the temporary situations that you are in and how a rash decision in a few seconds could destroy years or a lifetime of work.

7. Always start with a positive attitude. Whatever you do professionally, go in with a positive attitude. Start each day with thoughts about what you can accomplish rather than why it's so hard to accomplish something. If you start out with a defeatist attitude, you already know what you are going to get. If you start out with a positive attitude, you may surprise yourself with what you can achieve.

8. Give people the benefit of the doubt. Unless you've been on the other side, you may not always know what it's like to be talked about and criticized. Rather than repeat the same mistakes and get caught up in the negativity of others, give people the benefit of the doubt. Rather than believing the worst about people, believe in the possibility of the best.

9. Start with the end in mind. When we feel wronged by people it's so tempting for us to tell them off, to seek revenge or to take your marbles and go home. Instead, think about when this situation is all over and the truth has won, what do you want people to think about you? How do you want to feel about yourself? Design your responses, the way you carry yourself and how you treat people with the end result you desire in mind. Instead of cursing someone out, remember that this person could be your enemy now but could one day be your ally. Focus on the goal you've set out to achieve and not the little things that bother you.

13. Un-limit Yourself

ALTHOUGH IT'S TEMPTING TO BEGIN this chapter with what the dictionary says about success, I realize that it would contradict what I believe to be the most important principle about success, and that is, it is to be defined by you. Success is ageless and timeless. So often we choose arbitrary numbers and timelines and try to define ourselves by the attainment of those things. I'm not talking about setting goals that are measurable and have some timeline attached to them. Those are important things to do when you are trying to achieve something.

I'm talking about the little speech we give ourselves that, by the time we are thirty or whatever age, we will have the mate, the 2.5 children, and the house with a white picket fence. When things don't line up that way, we somehow believe we have failed. While we may want to be married by a particular age, our own success shouldn't be defined by the things we can't control. We may want to have a mate by a certain time, but what if we haven't found that person yet? What if the person we are with at that particular age isn't the person we are supposed to be with for the rest of our life? Success is not about arbitrary numbers and timelines. Success doesn't happen when you reach a certain age.

There are some who are incredibly successful and some who have never really met success because they aren't living to their fullest potential. Some people are still reaching for success. Success is not necessarily a destination. We have to get rid of the notions in our heads that success meets a particular standard, that when I get "there," or when I have those things, then I'll achieve success. I think success is who we become on the way to those goals. It's how we handle the situation when obstacles arise, how we treat other people, and how we treat ourselves. Success is the lessons we've learned and the skills we develop along the way and how we use them to reach our goals. It keeps us from making the same mistakes twice and makes habits of those things we did well to ensure that we do them over and over again.

Success is reaching the goals that have been set, both big and small, and ensuring that when you reach those goals you are reaching back to help someone else. It's freely sharing what you know with other people to help them in their journey. Success is also being at your personal best. It's not achieving what someone else deems great but achieving what is your personal best.

It's like being in school and you make straight A's and never have to pick up a book. If it's effortless for you, how much does it mean to you? On the other hand, look at the student who, without studying, is a D student. Each time he tries, he gets better and better. Eventually after studying and preparing, he makes an A in that class. That's success. It's also the person who has worked hard and earned a C. That's still success.

Success is working at your personal best to get to a particular place in life. It's not even the A or C on the test but what a person learns about himself and his abilities while getting there. When the next obstacle or goal comes, a successful person knows the way to get there because he's already proven it to himself. It's why, when we see people who have achieved incredible things in life keep moving toward the next thing, we wonder: why not stop there?

Why? Because only you know what's your personal best. Only you know what you are capable of doing. No one else can determine success for you. It has to be defined and measured by you. When we begin to define success for ourselves, we un-limit ourselves from the standards of others. Other people's goals and expectations can be great. It's not until we decide for ourselves what success looks like that we can commit to achieving it and then later determine if we have reached it.

Over the last few years, I have discovered that people on the outside are not qualified to determine what success is or isn't for you. They don't know your purpose in life or your skills and abilities, nor do they know the circumstances you operate in. How many times do we define success by money and the ability to amass material things? Yet, when we observe the behaviors of celebrities or high-profile individuals, we recognize their unhappiness or discontent, despite all the things and people they have in their lives. Success for them may be the achievement of a particular role or a certain bonus for signing with a sports team, but it is also about their lives and who they are aside from the dollar signs.

For us, success shouldn't be about the position we have attained in our line of work but about the person we have become and the people we have helped along the way. What good is success if you cannot share it with the people around you? What good is success if you have stepped all over the people behind you to get where you are? Success is the understanding that your achievements don't exist because of what someone else is not. It is the belief that reaching your goals is as attached to others as it is to you. Success is about those lessons you have learned along the way that will help you in your next endeavors, as well as the people who are trying to get to where you are. It is the belief that your good is not at the expense of someone else's bad.

When I was growing up and achieving certain awards or honors—for example, winning an oratorical contest in high school—I would be excited, of course. But even after winning the coveted award, I always got that feeling that it was time to do something else, something more. It wasn't for the praise, awards, or accolades. It was for me. It was because I knew there was more for me to do, more for me to achieve, more that I was capable of. I couldn't have articulated this at the time, but I knew what was possible for me.

The same is true now. Yes, I am blessed and have achieved great things by a lot of people's standards. I also know that there is even more for me to do and more for me to accomplish. It's not about attaining more awards or pats on the back; it's about knowing my personal best and my capacity to do more. Admittedly, it is kind of scary for us to think about what more we can do in our lives and in our communities. Former president of South Africa, Nelson Mandela made a moving statement: "Our deepest fear is not that we are inadequate. Our deepest fear is that we are powerful beyond measure." I believe success is the ability to escape fear and operate in what is possible for you.

Rather than defining my success in the legislature by how many bills I have passed or how high I can reach in leadership positions, my success is based on my purpose for getting into the political process in the first place, and that is to connect people with their government and get them more involved in the political process. When I set out to run for office, it was to serve as a conduit for the people in my community to better understand the process and better access the resources and information that is available to them. My purpose for being in the legislature was never based on the positions that I have acquired or the bills that are passed. Certainly, within the legislative process there are goals that are set to pass bills and acquire leadership positions. For some, that is their purpose, and success for them is based on how well they reach those appointed goals. They have set their own benchmarks and, based on their own prescribed accountability practices, they must determine if they have reached those goals.

Determining your success has to begin with understanding your purpose and why you have been called to do a particular thing, followed by knowledge of what you are trying to achieve while there. Sometimes your purpose for working at a particular company may have nothing to do with how far you climb the ladder to a specific position. Sometimes your purpose could be to learn and develop necessary skills you want to utilize in a totally different company or entity. Sometimes success could be based on the number of people you are able to touch because of your leadership style and your talent for encouraging others to be the best they can be. If you spend your time basing your success on what other people believe it should be or what the conventional wisdom says, you could find yourself feeling quite inadequate. When we base our success or failure on what other people say, we begin living our lives for someone else and not according to our own purpose.

There are some things that we don't consider when we talk about success. When we see individuals we deem successful, we mostly think about the things they have and where they are now. We don't realize there is a story behind their success that oftentimes is connected to some kind of adversity. We see successful businesspeople, but we don't know their stories of failed companies, homelessness, helplessness, or the obstacles they had to overcome to get where they are.

Sometimes we find success in our failures. I find that many "successful" people I talk to learn their most valuable lessons from their failures. In fact, it was often because of their failures that they learned how to succeed. It was their failures that developed their skill sets and taught them about the importance of having a good team. Failure taught them how to work from strong inner focus and strength and how to function with bare bones. I encourage you to do the research and learn about companies and individuals who have great stories to tell about the difficulties of getting to where they are. They have an appreciation for those roadblocks that helped them to get where they are.

We can learn lessons from those individuals in our own lives. What do we learn from the times when we didn't do well on a test, when we didn't get a strong evaluation at work, when we didn't get that business or home loan the first time, when we had a failed relationship? The powerful lessons we've learned from those experiences not only help to shape who we are, they help us to apply what we've learned to achieving success in those areas the next time. Those successes may not even come the second or third time, but, each time we try again, we learn something from the previous attempt. Each failure forces us to try yet another approach until we get to our desired destination.

We also rarely talk about the people around us who either help us get closer to our goals or who stand in the way. Success can depend on the people you choose to associate with. We all heard growing up that we should watch the company that we keep. As adults we sometimes forget that. Success says that we should want to surround ourselves with people who want to see us do well—the people who will support our dreams and ask what they can do to help them become a reality. It's important to find people whose values and mindsets are similar to our own. We can't choose our families, but we can certainly choose our friends, the environments we choose to dwell in, and the messages we allow ourselves to consume.

I believe successful people understand the importance of keeping people around them who will push them to get to the next level, inspire them, and even teach them. When we spend time with people who are moving in the same direction or have already reached the place we are trying to get to, we become more inspired. I am not suggesting that we dump our friends who may not be doing as well. I am suggesting that we find those people in our lives that can stretch us. I think success is also determined by who you are, and that can be reflected in who you hang out with.

This principle also applies to those individuals who don't want you to be successful, those who tell you how impossible it is to reach the goals you have set. They are simply haters. Haters are those who spend most of their time thinking about how something can't be done. Their energy zaps you of all inspiration and hope. We all know those people. Some are in our families, some are our spouses, and some are friends we have had for decades. Whoever they are, we must be conscious of the spaces we are in and the negative messages we absorb, words that tell us we can't, tell us we can't *now*, or constantly ask us how we are going to do something. Haters have issues in their own lives and their "stuff" permeates all aspects of their lives, including their interactions with you. They make it their business to stand in your way as roadblocks, and they will not stop until you fail. There are haters who simply want to talk about you behind your back or to your face. Their words cut like daggers because they are close to us. They are older, they are younger, they help perpetuate the generational gap, and they are our peers. Haters come in all forms. Our job is to ensure that they don't take up any room in our minds or hearts.

This is a time when you "make your haters your motivators." Rather than allowing those people to seep into your brain space, make the words, their negativity, their discouraging spirits, serve as motivators for you. The people who say you can't—show them how you can. Take those words and obstacles as the games we used to play as children when we dared each other to do something. Accept their hate as a license to exceed all expectations. Understand that whether you succeed or fail, it isn't based on what they say but whether you choose to listen. Sometimes those haters are people we love the most, and we wish that they, if no one else, would be the ones to encourage us. They can be our parents, our closest friends, even people we consider to be our mentors. We have to remain steadfast, focused on the goal at hand, and remember to use the obstacles, the haters, and the naysayers as stepping stones and even motivation.

I remember when I first ran for the legislature; there were so many haters along the way, such as the "advocate" for black women who left me messages on my voicemail about how I was going to lose to people along the way who just couldn't see success in their own lives and whose minds couldn't open to see mine. There were also individuals who were behind the residency challenge, whose tricks they counted on to count me out. The haters contributed symbolically to my campaign because they thought it was "cute" for me to run and that it would be a "nice experience."

There were so many along the way whose vision didn't extend where mine was. It was up to me to choose to either listen to them or use them as my stepping stones. It was up to me whether I would continue to hang out with them or make sure I spent as little time in their presence as possible. There have been haters who said my marriage wouldn't work, and even one or two people in my family who didn't think I would amount to much because no one around them had. We all have some negative element around us; the question is, what do we do with them?

Once you have succeeded in the goals you've set for yourself, some of those same haters will remain in your life. It's easy for us to want to rub it in their faces, to brag about how far we have come, and even to remind them about their wrongdoing. As much as we would like to seek revenge for all of the wrong people have done in our lives, I've found that success is the best revenge. You won't have to say or do anything; simply be who you are. Your success and your humility about it will speak for itself.

In fact, on more than one occasion, I have found that my position has enabled me to help the same people who told me it was impossible to win a legislative seat in Cobb County. The same woman who left me messages that I couldn't win, I honored one year at the capitol. There was no malice behind it. I was truly honoring her for the work she has done in the state for other black women, even if it wasn't for me. Because I understood that my success and my failure was in no way connected to her, I had the ability to see beyond her words and understand that her stuff had nothing to do with me.

It's the same for the guy who was going to be my campaign manager. I see him often at political functions in my county. I always greet him with a smile. In fact, I like seeing him, because I know I am walking in the manifestation of what success is when you make your haters your motivators. I am clear that he is an example of what happens when you keep your mind focused on the goals ahead and not on the people who have no bearing on whether you reach those goals.

No words or harmful deeds could ever satisfy a person's need for vengeance. It is not the payback that helps you feel better, it is the success that tells you and the other people that you can do anything you put your mind to. It is their conscience that will bother them because they know what they have done. The real revenge happens when you let go of your ill feelings toward them and enjoy the success that you have earned. Sometimes it's hard to do. If we are to be successful, we have to remember that the haters will always be there. It's not for us to allow them to have any power in our lives to affect the outcome one way or the other.

When we won the residency challenge in 2002, I couldn't help but want to go and shove the reversal order in the faces of those I knew were behind the challenge in the first place. When I won the race, I wanted to drive by the house of the guy who was my original campaign manager. Actually, we did. We drove by with four or five cars honking our horns. Looking back, of course, it was quite immature. We wanted a way to say, "Na na-na na na, look what we did." We wanted a way to pay him back for all of the time, money, and resources we had to pour into the legal challenge and for the lost time when I could have been out knocking on doors and getting more votes. Nothing would have made me feel better than to make him say he was sorry for all he and his cronies had done.

I had those thoughts for at least a few months—until I saw him at a public meeting. That was my opportunity to rub it in his face and give him a piece of my mind. He was standing with his wife and probably wished he could vanish into thin air. He looked uncomfortable; he was red in the face and was clearly hoping that I wouldn't say a word. And I didn't. What I realized at that moment was that my natural desire to get revenge—or to give him the sister girl, rolling-my-neck-and-eyes reprimand—wouldn't change the fact that we had prevailed and his candidate would have to find something else to do for at least the next two years. The truth is, I knew that his seeing me, still standing and with prize in hand, would be revenge enough.

That wouldn't be the last time I would see him. At least once he had to sit in an audience and hear about the triumphs in my life, especially the one he helped create. My success and prevailing through that situation was more revenge than I could ever imagine. Every time I see him, I smile, shake his hand, and genuinely ask how he is doing. I don't wish him any harm or bad karma, because going through that experience has literally changed my life. It changed how I see things and how I see God. It's an example that I can recall in my life, one that reminds me that there *will* be challenges, but that if I can get through that, I can get through the next one.

What is success for you? What goals have you set for yourself that are directly connected to who you are and the role you have been put in this place to fill? If you have been placed on this earth to teach, yet you are the CEO of a company, is your success based on the number of clients your company brings in or how many people you have mentored, coached, and taught the ropes along the way? Was this the job you were called to do in the first place? These are questions we should be able to answer so that our success is based on our purpose and unique reason for being on earth.

Success for me is being an effective legislator. It's passing more education legislation that will create opportunities for young people for generations to come. Success is being able to work across the aisle, bring the parties together, and ultimately bring more people into the process to make it work better for us all.

In my personal life, success is being a good wife to my husband, remaining his best friend, working hard to maintain a healthy and happy marriage, and having the ability to keep a smile on his face. Success is raising my daughter to be strong, bold, and smart. Success is teaching her to appreciate her many blessings and to understand the importance of what she was born to contribute to the world. Success is leaving a legacy that both she and my stepson Rashaan can be proud of.

Success is being able to be good to my parents, especially my mother, in return for all of the many sacrifices she made so that I can be who I am. Success for me is living my life on purpose. It's making choices for life that bring happiness and pure joy. Its living life with no regrets and being proud of who I am.

A recent success for me was the process of writing and now publishing this book. It is pouring my heart into a project so that I could sow positive seeds in the lives of people, especially young women. Success would be selling a great number of them and speaking to groups all over the country. A greater success would be touching the lives of people like you who will take these words to heart and apply them to your life. Success is knowing that I gave this my all in the hopes of inspiring, challenging, and provoking thought, ideas, and action.

❖ LESSONS I LEARNED ALONG THE WAY ❖

1. Never apologize for defining success for yourself. Set your own benchmarks and your own ideas of what success is. It's not success if it's the definition of what other people deem is success for you.

2. Success is about fulfillment as much as it about attainment. When we set out to reach a particular position, our real success is in the lessons we learn and how they make us better. It's setting meaningful goals that serve a purpose larger than you.

3. Success is about doing your personal best. Only you know what your personal best is. Set your standards based upon what you know you are capable of.

4. Pay attention to the person you become on your way to success. Just as we learn from the challenges in our lives, we also learn from our successes. Seize those moments to learn and teach others. How do you better the world and the people around you because of what you have accomplished? How much have you given back of what you've received?

5. It's not a matter of if, but how. It's not what happens to you but how you respond to it that prepares you for success. We have all heard the expression about making lemonade out of lemons. We all face challenges. It's what we do with those challenges that help us in our quest to success. Successful people learn how to stay focused on the goal at hand and not allow bumps in the road to keep them away from their destiny. It's how we handle both triumph and hardship that determine how much success we have.

6. Find people you deem successful and compare their habits. What things can you learn from successful people? What are the common personality traits, daily habits, advice, regimen, people, or organizations they associate with? While we should define success for ourselves, there are important lessons we can learn from people who are considered successful.

7. Success is the best revenge. Stop wasting your time wondering how you are going to pay back your haters. Roadblocks—whether people or problems—help us to become stronger. The best way to pay people back for standing in your way and telling you how much you can't do is to do it and do it well. Seeking revenge or paying them back for all they've done takes precious time away from you reaching your highest potential.

14. LESSONS THAT TRANSCEND THROUGH LIFE, LOVE, AND POLITICS

1. Maintain meaningful relationships with people. Whether it's the job you want to secure, the person you want to do something for you, or the bill you want passed, it often comes down to relationships. Take time to get to know people for who they are, not just what they can do for you. Understand that it's your meaningful relationships with people that make it easier or more difficult to achieve your end goal. Find ways to cultivate relationships with the people you want in your life.

Whether it's making sure they are on your Christmas list, sending out regular e-mails, scheduling coffee or a meal, or always doing your best to help people when they have a specific need, invest time getting to know who people are and how you can add to one another's lives. There will be times when your degrees, your wit, and your experience aren't enough. It will come down to who you know and who knows you. Never underestimate the power of relationships and how they can help you move closer to your purpose.

2. Become a lifelong learner. As we go through life, it's easy to be comfortable, even complacent with where we are. We should always remember that, just as we look at certain groups of people and ask why they don't do more for themselves, we should ask ourselves the same question. Take on learning a new language or learn more about yourself. Never become content with what you know. We should do our best to stretch ourselves and expose ourselves to new things. Becoming a lifelong learner means the world remains open to you, as do the possibilities of what it has to offer. We have all heard that we use so little of our brains. What we've been given, let's use. Learn all that life has to teach us through books, other people, classes, or technology. Take full advantage of the resources that are often right at our fingertips.

3. Become a mentor. How often have we complained that we have no one to teach us the ropes for our particular line of work? Let's not repeat that cycle. Becoming a mentor provides you the opportunity to open doors for others and take those coming up behind you under your wings. Teaching those who may not know as much as we do about life or a particular area of interest also gives us the opportunity to do some learning for ourselves. There are plenty of people who would love to know what you know. Find them or let them find you, and give them the gift of mentorship.

4. Serve others. Winston Churchill once said, "We make a living by what we get; we make a life by what we give." No matter what your purpose is, we are all called to serve. Marian Wright Edelman said, "Service is the rent we pay for living on this earth." Life should be about what you give to others. When we serve others, we forget about our own issues and challenges. There is a great feeling we get when we serve others. It is the satisfaction of knowing that you were able to do something for someone who couldn't do it for him or herself. The human race is a great species. Dr. King said, "We can all be great because we can all serve." Imagine what the world would be like if we focused on serving others before serving ourselves. Even in marriage, when each person is focused on serving the other, all needs are met.

5. Take time to appreciate the simple things in life. Sometimes we get caught up in our problems, our big situations, even our big titles. Never cease thanking God for the ability to breathe, use your limbs, or think. Never cease to appreciate the people around you who are a part of your life. Whether it's your significant other, family, or team at work, take a moment to thank them for who they are and the value they add to your life. When we get caught up in the big things, we forget about the small things that make our worlds go 'round. Never take for granted these things, as none of them are promised to us forever.

6. Don't live a life in regret. We have all made mistakes that we wish we could do over. The fact is, most times we can't. What we can do is learn from the mistakes and bad decisions that we have made in the past and become better prepared for our next opportunity to make a better decision. I once heard a preacher ask why the windshield of a car is so much bigger than the rearview mirror. He said it's for us to spend a lot more time looking forward than looking back. We have to forgive ourselves for the mistakes we made yesterday and figure out how to make the best life we can today. Holding onto hurts and guilt can't change the situation or give you back the time you waste mulling over it. As long as you are still breathing, you have time to create the life you want, and that shouldn't be one filled with regret. Learn to let go.

7. Become a goal setter. Every day you wake up, you ought to have goals that you set for yourself. Take the time to write them down, hold yourself accountable, and check them off at the end of the day. Setting smaller goals helps you get to your bigger goals. Take it one step at a time. It's like having a roadmap to help you figure out how to get from one place to another.

8. Live life without limits. The most successful people we know got there because they didn't allow the odds, the lack of a path, or haters to keep them away from their destiny. Start living your life from a place of *why you can* rather than *why you can't* or *why it's so hard*. In life, in marriage or relationships, and in politics, never let anyone define what is possible and impossible for you. Only you can determine how far you will go, based on your determination and belief that anything is possible. Living a life without limits gives you the best that life has to offer, because you aren't bogged down in the never-ending excuses of why not. Live and let live. Enjoy each day, living it to the fullest. Once you set your goals, give it your all and don't let anyone, including you, get in the way.

9. Do it now. How many of us know people who are always saying what they want to do, what they should do, and what they are getting ready to do? Do you notice that they never actually do it? Resolve in your mind that what you want can happen if you *do* it rather than talk about doing it. Stop spending your energy "preparing" for what you want to do; just go ahead and do it. Waiting for the right time, the right spouse, the right amount of money, or the right opportunity leaves us doing just that—waiting. Decide what you want, how you will get there, and jump in and do it.

10. Never apologize for who you are. How could I *not* end with this very important point? Always remember that God created you to be who you are. He did not create us to replicate what He has done in someone else. Being our authentic selves helps other people to respect who we are rather than to be confused by who they (and we) *thought* we were. You are the sum of your life experiences. Whether they are good or bad, your perspective is shaped by your journey. This doesn't mean to treat people badly because that's the way you were treated. It means to treat people well because you know what it feels like to be treated badly and you wouldn't want others to feel that pain—and make no apologies for it. Stand up for yourself and for others because that's the right thing to do. Even if there are consequences for those actions, the principles we live will outweigh any job, position, or relationship. When you refuse to apologize for wanting the best for yourself and for other people, your blessings will come twofold.

I wish you the best life possible, and live it with *no apologies!*

For more information about Alisha Thomas Morgan, her products and services, or to book speaking engagements, visit www.noapologiesbook.com

Stay connected, and follow her at www.facebook.com/ alishathomasmorgan and www.twitter.com/@alishamorgan